D1171288

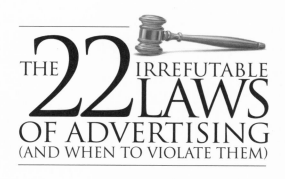

THE 22 IRREFUTABLE LAWS OF ADVERTISING
(AND WHEN TO VIOLATE THEM)

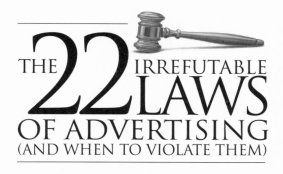

THE 22 IRREFUTABLE LAWS OF ADVERTISING (AND WHEN TO VIOLATE THEM)

MICHAEL NEWMAN.

John Wiley & Sons (Asia) Pte Ltd

Other Wiley Editorial Offices
John Wiley & Sons, Inc., 111 River Street, Hoboken, NJ 07030, USA
John Wiley & Sons Ltd, The Atrium, Southern Gate, Chichester PO19 BSQ, England
John Wiley & Sons (Canada) Ltd, 22 Worcester Road, Rexdale, Ontario M9W ILI, Canada
John Wiley & Sons Australia Ltd, 33 Park Road (PO Box 1226), Milton, Queensland 4046, Australia
Wiley-VCH, Pappelallee 3, 69469 Weinheim, Germany

Library of Congress Cataloging-in-Publication Data:

0470-82106-x

Typeset in 11/15 point, Garamond by Red Planet
Printed in Singapore by Saik Wah Press Pte Ltd
10 9 8 7 6 5 4 3 2 1

CONTENTS

This book is dedicated to Steve Costello;
who taught me that you can be a Law unto yourself,
and still have the greatest curiosity, compassion and gentle bonhomie.

ACKNOWLEDGEMENTS

I'd like to acknowledge my publisher, Nick Wallwork, for his patience with this sprawling project, with me, and this unwieldy and overarching idea.

Thanks also to Michael at *Campaign Brief* and Patsy at *FBI* for their suggestions, as well as the passionate people at the Young Guns award. Danny Searle, Neil Lawrence and Garry Horner deserve thanks for trying to line up their particular corporations' gurus.

Special appreciation not only to the brilliant and generous contributors, but particularly to the tireless advertising PAs of the world, who bore the brunt of daily missives and juggled impossible schedules.

Also, to the couple of advertising gurus who over-promised and under-delivered (the very opposite philosophy to what is espoused in this book) – so were left out of this project – I'd like to acknowledge that you've been outclassed by your peers.

Thanks to Jennifer Eborall, as always, for her clearheaded design.

And lastly, thanks to my clients, workmates and loved ones who've cheerfully put up with yet another book, written within yet another year, that's dominated too much of my time and attention.

You all deserve better.

Mike Newman and I were once a creative team. For nearly eight years I relied on his ability to rearrange the alphabet into words that touch the senses. Our goal together was to create ads that make an emotional connection. Even if our efforts sometimes attracted an over-emotional response, for example, the client who threatened to burn our agency down, and turn it into a restaurant. At our best our work won major accounts and major awards.

At our worst we wrote a TV spot for a feminine hygiene product that featured a dam.

You do learn from experience.

And this book is the opportunity to learn from 22 of the most experienced practitioners in the business.

"When you've got a good fact, get out of the way" is a tip we picked up from the legendary Dave Trott.

And as you'll see, Mike gets out of the way to let the contributors speak to you, one on one, about the irrefutable laws of advertising. Frankly, I don't know how Mike persuaded all these heavy hitters to participate. Perhaps they were all thinking, as I did when I rushed at the chance to write this foreword:

"Wow, imagine being in a book with those guys!"

When Mike and I worked together, one of our clients had a big sign on his wall which read: "WIIFM."

It stood for 'What's In It For Me?'

It was the question we knew we would have to answer with every ad we presented.

I suspect it was the starting place for Mike with this book. Cleverly, the "What's In It For Me?" he presents here is an irrefutable ad proposition.

22 books for the price of one!

Bob Isherwood
Worldwide Creative Director
Saatchi & Saatchi

THE RULES OF ENGAGEMENT

I rrefutable, immutable, incontrovertible, indubitable, indisputable, incontestable – big promise is the heart of advertising. But the really big word in this book's title is "Laws."

Laws and advertising have always been a problematic combination. The words initially seem to go together as evidently as vodka and wheat grass (used to).

Advertising, surely, is maverick. Thriving on the never seen before. Shunning formulae. Dismissive of rules.

How can advertising, the most ephemeral of all business expenses, have laws in a practical way that, say, mathematics or physics does?

The Law of the Jungle, some might say.

Or Murphy's Law?

Or worse, the Law of Diminishing Returns?

And surely the edgy world of the agency's creative department will cringe at the notion of something as restrictive as universal rules.

They might suspect something squeezed within these covers may limit where their creative ejaculations might flow next. To them I say, think of these 22 chapters not as laws of nature to be obeyed, but as forces of nature to be used to your advantage.

Fury + Control = Genius.

This book is not about rules to be waved as a stick to kill off ideas. Nor are they failsafe, pithy prescriptions. Unfortunately, "the likelihood of discovering a foolproof formula for successful advertising is about as realistic as finding the formula for living life" to quote a down-to-earth colleague of mine, Australian TV pundit, Jane Caro. Rather, we have set it out as a simple guide to the fundamentals of successful commercial communication.

The project's modest objective is to codify the primary universal principles of effective advertising, as nominated by the world's top practitioners: from every corner of the globe. The principles of marketing have been overlaid with any number of architectural models to guide practitioners (brand temples, ladders, onions, molecular charts, cartwheel models) in the past. Until now, the advertising end of the marketing process has been less well analysed.

Advertising creativity is seen as an uncertain force, residing not in neat, identifiable and quantifiable processes, but rather gut feel, so called "super-logic," creative intuition and God-given-luck.

Some years ago, I met Roy Grace, the legendary New York art director, who apparently experienced his intuitive signals quite physically. When asked how he knew that the idea he'd come up with was a genuine killer, he simply answered: "My balls tingle."

How to catch lightning in a bottle

Is everything really that relative? Every decision so subjective? Is the truth just personal opinion? Creative anarchy?

Was success ever more than a happy knack for knowing where good opportunities exist, and having a sense about which ones will respond to imagination?

Until you peel back the layers, creating great advertising seems an esoteric exercise. But like it or not, marketing needs a creative leap before it can reach into people's hearts.

So, how do we jump from the earnest conventionality of the boardroom's world of facts and figures, into the lively realm of imagination, with confidence?

This book seeks to help resolve that. Luminaries from around the globe have gathered together for this project, for the first time, to spell out the practical magic that's made their advertising so successful; to elucidate the mystery and clarify a useful roadmap to the future. Follow the counsel of these leading lights and you'll make more subtle, intuitive, percipient judgements about your advertising.

New knowledge comes from solving problems; the most valuable knowledge is called tacit knowledge — tacit because it has been embedded through experience; learnt, and not written down. Access to those with specialised tacit wisdom is scarce and highly valuable in this knowledge economy.

The distinguished and learned judging panel has been elected for the breadth of their reputations, the far-sightedness of their current work, the spectacular success of their clients (and their own companies), as well as the balance of views from the US, UK, Europe, South Africa, South America, Southeast Asia and Australasia.

No regard has been taken to represent certain agency networks over others; we're not claiming to be politically correct. (Just correct.) This is not a guide to which agency should pitch for your advertising business next time around, rather for what you should look for in any advertising that you expect to be successful in the future.

Of course, the interpretation of each Law is that of the individual contributor and, no doubt, not everyone involved will completely share all of the opinions expressed. Indeed, paradoxical attitudes and differing styles are part of the vivacity of the text. Rather, it is the examination of the underlying principles of great advertising that's the task at hand.

Nobel Prize winning author, Patrick White, once wrote about the concept of "creative reason"; that phrase may strike a right chord here — a discussion of the creative imagination as a particular form of thought, with a demanding logic of its own. We're trying to shine a spotlight on what is important to encourage in successful advertising, as well as point out what transgressions should be avoided at all cost.

Why precisely 22, you may ask? (But then, why the Famous Five, the Secret Seven, the Fab Four?). It's not just alliteration. It's a magic number.

This book is a re-generation, indeed reinvention, of the series that began with the 22 Laws of Marketing and of Branding, that were variously examined in the profoundly influential works of Messrs Trout, Ries and Ms Ries. Now it's advertising's turn.

Are there other irrefutable laws beyond these 22? Yes, no doubt, and the search will continue at the project website: The22lawsofadvertising.com

How bad is it, doc?

Never in its glittering history has advertising so needed its global stars to show guidance — there have been dark days in most markets recently; indeed, the world has changed too fast for many businesses. The psychological landscape has shifted seismically in every nation on earth during the last few years, just as media fragmentation has cracked the windscreen of many business prime movers. The result has been carnage in many industries. Even established products have crashed and burned in the new marketplace.

Yet many agencies today still cling to old ways, and allow their clients to spend millions careening down known dead ends that are already littered with me-too wrecks. Or, just as reprehensively, to launch themsselves so completely overloaded with baggage that their struggling campaigns have no chance of reaching their target audience alive. Little wonder the advertising business has been struggling through its worst recession in 70 years.

(In 2003, Standard & Poor's index of global advertising companies fell 20% in the first three months and was down 70% from its peak in December 1999. Advertising was the worst performing industry only behind tobacco [Sydney Morning Herald/Deutsch Bank, March 03].)

Media has fragmented.

Cynical and increasingly savvy consumers have rebelled.

Mainstream agencies have lost ground to direct marketers. (At the time of writing, Deutsch Bank cautiously forecast a long-term growth trend of 5% pa for advertising agencies, beside a 6 to 8% growth in non-traditional marketing.)

At the same time, many clients lost their (blind) faith in the power of advertising. Belief just died out.

Or was it murder?

Has the ever-zealous research industry been an accomplice before the fact? (The jury's still out on that one.)

Either way, someone looked up "advertising" in their dictionary and stumbled on another word that was far sexier to CEOs, CFOs and shareholders:

"Accountability."

Everything since then has conspired against advertising as it used to be.

Retrenchments sapped the industry's will.

Research drained its originality.

Reality has outdone its special effects.

Frankly, it's no surprise that marketers are reapportioning funds. The average marketing director, after all, has of late been having a pretty savage time of it too.

Slashed budgets have been imposed at the same time as sluggish demand and increased competition; short-term, tactical strategies have been the usual knee-jerk reaction, with quarterly sales charts and at-all-cost profit growth the order of the day, all at the expense of long-term revenue development.

Companies have learned that they don't have to fail to go extinct.

They just have to succeed less often than their competitors. The CEO of one famous advertising agency recently summed it up to me like this: "The anti-Christ has won."

Clearly, then, there's never been a better time for this book.

Success symbols

Great advertising is created through a combination of deep analytical skills with the subtle nuances of our truest blood-nature.

Advertising is wilful imagination. Applied to marketing. It's a discipline. The only art is in the creation of symbols and stories that catch the fundamental truths of everyday life.

Success means learning to engage, fascinate, hold and, thereby, profit from these symbols and stories. Look at what follows as the rules of engagement.

Today's advertising process is often fraught, riddled with dead ends, a maze of contradictions and precipitous paths, well-worn tracks and pedestrian solutions. In reality, it's a craft, more like a medieval stonemason's workshop (except that stone is easier to crack than a truly persuasive idea.) Advertising's role is as a transmitting device between marketing and consumer — it translates rational marketing into a different and more compelling language.

Into the dialect of the emotions, the fears, spirit and even the funny bone. Great advertising is at once personal and universal, drawing people together in a shared experience.

At its best, it can resonate deeply; it says to people: "You are not alone." And when it's done with enough inspiration, like great pop music, it elevates its success to something more like art.

It enters our hearts.

It enters the lexicon.

It enters popular culture.

And it sells shiploads and shed loads of stuff, which is, after all, the whole idea of having an "advertising idea" in the first place.

This sounds obvious, but it's often forgotten in these exciting days of whiz bang production effects and brand strategies for the sake of brand consultants.

Great advertising also allows a brand to punch well above its weight. Great ads will transcend ordinary strategies, as well as inadequate budgets.

From the earliest stirrings of human self-awareness as a sentient species, our programmed cerebrums have sought to surround us with "meaning," through symbols. We crave them. Now, without being too deep too early in the book, it must be recognised that brands have become a major source of these succouring symbols for people in the 21st century. Indeed, a recent American study showed the rise in the use of brand names as Christian names: Canon, Bentley, Jaguar, Chanel, Porsche, Timberland, Reebok and even Xerox and Camry — you might also like to know there were 24 children called Unique.

Great advertising is the most profound way for companies to transform products into brands, and create that necessary symbolism.

It moves a marketer out of the rat race and into the brand-race.

Not brand for the sake of brand, or sleek egos.

But for the sake of greater sales, higher revenue and better profits.

The position this book takes is very simple.

A great advertising idea is the fastest and most cost effective tool in the fight to make more money by selling more product.

The "idea", of course, may not be an ad in the traditional sense, anymore. It should, in fact, be *an idea demonstrably bigger than an ad.*

The other starting point is that by the word "creative" I mean a way of communicating an idea that is inherently interesting to the target audience, and therefore essentially cheaper to run than the kind of advertisement that doesn't attract such attention.

"Creativity" gives marketing the power of persuasive immediacy. Which means the message cuts through faster and therefore costs less to run than an ordinary advertisement. An investment in great creativity saves big money when it comes to frequency. Which is a good beginning.

But that's all it is. More than impactful creativity is needed for success, otherwise there'd be only one Law to discuss.

People power

The day I wrote this Introduction, I came across a calculation which stipulated that within a couple of years' time, consumers will be pummelled with an average 1.3 marketing messages every waking second (Stephen Byrne, Diffusion *Jupiter Media Metrix*). I wonder how much benefit that "point 3" of a message would be to its advertiser? Perhaps you could even question the true value of the "1" complete message, that was about to be chased away by another 1.3 messages a second later?

The science of marketing has relied on the artful use of the 30-second TV advertisement (and in many creative departments, writers and art directors still while away their day writing scripts that begin: "The commercial opens on a beach in the Bahamas...")

But today, a great advertising idea must be bigger than an ad. Outside the square and beyond the media box.

A plethora of new-media is opening up possibilities for a brave new world of agency and clients to use — interactivity, virtual reality, so-called ambient and immersion techniques.

But it may be asked if all this is actually in danger of compounding the crime? At a rate of 1.3 messages per second, we'll already be pretty immersed. Stay immersed long enough and you drown. Clients today are worried about new ad filter technology attached to peoples' TV sets, without realising that people have actually already developed highly effective ad-filtering technology inside their brains some time back.

Recent studies indicate that both companies and their ads are failing to meet the needs of an increasingly dissatisfied and suspicious consumer. It's not just that people are becoming anti-advertising because of the sheer amount of it.

They're also objecting to the kind of advertising companies are making. Most people in developed markets see advertising as boring and repetitious. This repetitiveness is not about frequency per se, it also relates to sameness of execution style and message. Companies are doing little to be more engaging, and even though there's a deepening sense of anxiety in the marketplace, companies are still seen to be more interested in peddling their wares, rather than offering their customers solutions.

In short, most marketers are going about advertising wrong headedly.

People are not only turning advertising off, advertising itself is turning people off.

Each year, studies show *that more and more people are taking less and less notice* of ads than the previous year. It was 81% in 2003.

Advertisers must learn to change their behaviour if they want to influence purchasing behaviour: remember a lack of IQ is scientifically inferred if you keep failing to solve a problem by using the same method.

People want innovation from their corporations and their brands. And they're telling us that they're not getting it.

65% don't trust big companies anymore.

56% don't like global ads just because they are recognisably global.

69% think big companies have no ethics, *Grey Australia 2003*, quoted in May 29, *Business Review Weekly*.

Perhaps even more of a shock to some advertisers will be the consumer's accusation that creative standards are slipping.

No point arguing, the people are the ultimate jury.

What's the verdict?

Well, 71% of consumers say ads need to be more "outrageous and surprising" to catch their attention. They also advise finding "new and interesting ways" to communicate, promising they'll take more notice of ads if they appear where they're least expected.

Who'd have thought? Gosh, people want more stimulating relationships with us. No longer is it "Where's the beef?" Now, it's "Where's the idea, where's the fun, where's the innovation?"

Brands and their advertising are not leading the way, even though that's what consumers want us to do.

"Inventiveness" is seen as the most desirable quality in a company, said an outstanding 96% of Australian consumers in a recent study.

A recent Edelman UK survey found that advertising is the single least credible source of information, according to consumers. They don't want any more "messages"; they want respect, emotion, and genuineness. They don't want to learn about your product features; they want entertainment, empathy, and engagement.

The research industry has spent so much time rounding off the edges of creative advertising, it's ironic the latest studies say consumers want edgier advertising.

Bottom line is, people are no longer interested in the type of advertising that clients have done for decades.

They want stories. Not sales spiels.

A page is being turned in world advertising.

A short story

Once upon a time, on a country road, outside a one-street town called Koonoomoo, there were two strawberry farms. One on the left of the highway. One on the right.

To attract more of the passing trade his way, one of the farmers erected a sign beside the road, saying: *"Strawberry Farm."*

The competition on the other side then put up their own sign, and added a sense of immediacy: *"Strawberry Farm, now open."*

Not to be outdone, the first farmer changed his sign to add a new appeal: *"Strawberry Farm, now open. Pick your own."*

The opposition then rammed home their biggest and most logical advantage, ease of access and proximity: *"Strawberry Farm, now open. Pick your own – 300 metres."*

This flummoxed the farmer across the road; his strawberry patch was a good couple of miles away; way down an unmade dusty track, winding along a lonely bush creek. What to do?

His solution was to sell the emotional journey: *"Strawberry Farm – Scenic Drive."*

Enjoy the trip.

Michael Newman
February 2004

THE LAWGIVERS

Jim Aitchison, former executive creative director of the Batey Ad Group, gave up a very successful 20-year advertising career to pursue his passion for writing books. The result is the best selling *Cutting Edge Advertising/Television/Radio* series, *How Asia Advertises*, the *Clueless in Advertising/Public Relations/Banking and Finance/Marketing Communications/Starting a Business* series, the playful *Sarong Party Girl* series and, in 2003, *Is Anybody Out There? — The New Blueprint for Marketing Communications in the 21st Century.*

An Australian living in Singapore, he's a sought-after speaker and well-known radio personality and actor.

Jamie Barrett began his creative career at Fallon's famous Minneapolis agency in the US. In New York, he joined TBWA Chiat/Day for a year and then moved on to Wieden & Kennedy in Portland to work on Nike. Over the course of eight years there, he produced landmark work for Michael Jordan, Charles Barkley, Tiger Woods, tennis superstars Andre Agassi and Pete Sampras, and the Atlanta Olympics. He then returned to Fallon to lead their office in New York for three years, winning four gold Lions in the process. He is now creative boss at the legendary San Francisco agency, Goodby Silverstein & Partners.

Ian Batey was born in England and schooled in Australia. He's the founder of Singapore's Batey Ads Ltd which became Asia's largest independent agency network. Famed for its creation of the Singapore Airlines campaign, the agency is associated with many of Southeast Asia's primary brands. His agency credo preached advertising that "tickles the toes rather than the head."

His book, *Asian Branding,* was a business bestseller throughout the region.

Anne Bologna is president of Fallon, New York. Prior to this, she spent nearly 10 years at Fallon Minneapolis, most recently as head of strategic planning for some of the world's most respected brands: Starbucks, BMW, United Airlines, and Citibank, among them.

In 1998, she created the Starbucks brand bible, lending strategic focus in an entrepreneurial organisation on everything from product development to merchandising to marketing. She is a guest lecturer at the Harvard Business School and has taught marketing and consumer behaviour at St Thomas University.

Reg Bryson was a founding member of the creative icon agency brand, The Campaign Palace, in Sydney, and was chief executive until 2003. He was the first to introduce strategic planning as a discipline to the advertising industry in Australia.

His creative credits include ATV Ad of the Year and Cannes Gold. His strategic credits include more Australasian effectiveness awards than anyone else in the industry and was named an advertising living legend by *Campaign Brief*.

Jean-Marie Dru is president and CEO of TBWA Worldwide. He started as an account executive on the giant Procter & Gamble account at the Dupuy Compton agency in Paris in the 1970s, and progressed to become executive creative director in 1977. In the 1980s, he co-founded BDDP, which in 1988 merged with TBWA.

His books, *Disruption* and *Beyond Disruption*, have been influential bestsellers around the world, and he's twice been president of the Cannes Advertising Film Festival jury, in 1993 and 1998.

Neil French is worldwide creative director for Ogilvy & Mather. His ads were the first Asian campaigns to appear in the international award annuals. An Englishman, he brought a natural irreverence that transformed the somewhat proper Singapore advertising style and practically handmade the new Asian creativity.

He started as an account executive in his youth (he explains, that when times are hard you'll do anything for money).

Bob Isherwood was born and educated in Melbourne. He joined London agency CDP in their halcyon days and later became co-creative director of both Australia's The Campaign Palace and at Saatchi & Saatchi in Sydney, where he partnered the author. He is currently worldwide creative director of Saatchi & Saatchi, based in New York. In 2001, he acted as president of the Cannes Festival jury.

James Lowther is founding partner and now chairman of M&C Saatchi, London. He joined the original Saatchi & Saatchi as a copywriter in 1977, becoming joint creative director in 1987 and deputy chairman in 1989. All of which is no mean feat for someone whose first job was on a sheep station in the outback of Australia.

David Lubars, a Brooklyn, New York native, is currently president and executive creative director for Fallon, North America; he also serves on their worldwide board and management committee. Prior to this, he was CEO and chief creative officer of BBDO West.

He has won every major creative award in the world, including Gold and the inaugural Titanium at Cannes, Grand Clio, Grand ANDY, Gold One Show, Gold Effie, D&AD, and Communication Arts. He has twice appeared on the cover of *Archive* magazine.

Michael Newman studied Law before, happily, advertising discovered him. Some years later, he became Executive Creative Director of Saatchi & Saatchi in Australia, during their most creatively successful and biggest growth years; he sat on their worldwide creative board until late 2001, when he formed the ideas company, brandnewman.

He's a regular columnist in trade magazines across several different countries, and has toured and lectured on advertising subjects as far afield as South East Asia and South America.

In December 2003, he launched M&C Saatchi's second agency network, DNA, in Australia.

He is author of the advertising book, *Creative Leaps* (John Wiley & Sons, 2002).

Mike O'Sullivan is an Irishman who began his advertising career at Y&R London, before transferring to the Auckland office in 1994. In 1998, he was appointed executive creative director at New Zealand's largest agency, Colenso/BBDO, Auckland. He's been rewarded with eight Cannes Lions, five One Show pencils, three Effies, four NBR (Financial Times) Agency of the Year awards, and three out of four *Campaign Brief* Agency of the Year awards. He is ranked 7th in Asia's Top 10 creatives listing by *Media Magazine*, and *Campaign Brief* has just ranked him number one creative director in Australasia. In late 2003, he moved to Clemenger/BBDO, Melbourne.

MT Rainey is chairman of Rainey Kelly Campbell Roalfe/Y&R, the 6th largest agency in the UK. She is a planner by training and pioneered the discipline in the US at Chiat/Day in the 1980s. A graduate of Glasgow University, Mary Teresa is a regular speaker and publisher on communication and industry issues. She championed the move away from commission-based income to the notion of agencies charging for ideas and intellectual property. She chairs the Marketing Group of Great Britain and is a founding woman member of the 30 Club.

Al Ries is a legendary marketing strategist, renowned speaker and bestselling author. He first coined the concept of "positioning" more than 20 years ago. With marketing expert Jack Trout, he authored *Positioning: The Battle for Your Mind*, and followed up with *Marketing Warfare, Bottom-up Marketing, The 22 Immutable Laws of Branding*, and *Focus*, among others. With his daughter, Laura Ries, he collaborated to write *The 11 Immutable Laws of Internet Branding* and *The Fall of Advertising and the Rise of PR*, which was released in 2002.

He is co-founder and chairman of Atlanta-based marketing firm Ries and Ries.

Kevin Roberts was born in Lancaster in the north of England and started his advertising career as a marketing executive at Gillette and Procter & Gamble, before becoming CEO at Pepsi in the Middle East and later, Canada. He then moved to New Zealand to take up the post of chief operating officer for brewer, Lion Nathan.

In 1997, he joined Saatchi & Saatchi in New York as CEO worldwide. He is the inaugural CEO-in-residence at Cambridge University's business school and is co-author of *Peak Performance*, a business study of elite sporting organisations.

Allen Rosenshine was born in New York City and graduated from Columbia College. He's now chairman and CEO of BBDO Worldwide Inc. He's been recognised by *Advertising Age* as one of the 100 most influential people in advertising over the past century. In 1986, he spearheaded the creation of Omnicom Group, now one of the largest and most successful marketing communications companies in the world. He then rejoined BBDO as chairman and chief executive officer. Most recently, in 2000 and 2001, *Ad Age Global* named BBDO Global Agency Network of the Year, an honour never bestowed on any other agency for two successive years.

He was president of the jury at the 1991 International Advertising Festival of Cannes.

Marcello Serpa is joint CEO and creative director at Almap/BBDO, Brazil. Born in Rio de Janeiro, he studied visual and graphic art in Munich. He worked at GGK Düsseldorf and RG Wiesmeier before returning to Brazil and agencies DPZ and DM9.

His work has variously won the Grand Prix at Cannes, Clio, New York Festival and he was the first Brazilian to become president of the London Festival in 1998. He was president of the Cannes Festival jury in 2000 and has been a Cannes Lion winner 48 times. And counting.

John Shaw is based in Hong Kong and is regional planning director at O&M, leading a team of 60 — reputed to be the largest such group in the Asia Pacific.

Previously, he has worked in the UK and US, on brands such as Nike, Coke and Microsoft, at agencies Wieden+Kennedy and Young & Rubicam, London.

Kash Shree is senior vice president/creative director at Leo Burnett USA, in Chicago. Most recently, his Nike "Tag" commercial picked up the 2002 Grand Prix at Cannes; his "Play" campaign also won a Gold and Bronze Lion, as well as D&AD, One Show, Clio, Andy Awards and the Art Directors Club of New York awards. Prior to this, he worked as a copywriter at Wieden & Kennedy.

He was born in Singapore, raised and educated in England, and earned his Bachelor's in graphic design from the Kent Institute of Design in 1990.

Dave Trott was born in Barking, England, and graduated from a scholarship to art school in New York. He joined the creative department of UK agency BMP in 1971. In 1980, he founded the London hotshop GGT. In 1990, he started BST. In between, he became an inspiration and hero to a generation of young creatives.

He is now creative director of Walsh, Trott, Chick, & Smith.

Sebastian Turner is CEO and creative director of Berlin's Scholz & Friends, Europe's largest independent agency network, with 800 people in 18 countries. He serves as honorary professor at the Berlin University of Fine Arts and as president of the German Art Directors Club. He was the first German president of the Clio jury and has won Adman of the Year as well as Campaign of the Century.

His book *Spring!* (*Jump!* in English) is an advertising best seller.

Jack Vaughan has been named Australia's best advertising writer. He was the first to be elected to the AWARD Hall of Fame, the ATV Hall of Fame, and Campaign Brief's "THE WORK" Hall of Fame. He has collected shelves of local and international awards (including One Show, Clio and Cannes Gold) and been creative director of The Campaign Palace and Young & Rubicam, both in Australia and the UK and Australia's then largest advertising agency, George Patterson Bates, before co-founding Principals, a strategic and creative resource.

Most recently, he has become a "consultant collaborator" to other agencies, preferring to focus on his first love; solving creative and brand problems.

Graham V. Warsop, chairman and executive creative director of South Africa's The Jupiter Drawing Room, is an Englishman, with a legal background. He is a qualified barrister with a Masters in law from Cambridge University. Leaving the legal profession at age 28, he took on a job as a junior copywriter in an advertising agency in South Africa. Eighteen months later, he founded The Jupiter Drawing Room, named after a brothel in a Guy de Maupassant short story.

As creative director, his awards include, in 2001 alone, five Cannes Lions, three One Show, and five Clio Magazine Best of Show at the New York Festivals.

Advertising Age's Creativity magazine, in its most recent creativity survey, ranked The Jupiter Drawing Room the fifth most creative agency in the world—the first time an African agency has ever made it into the global Top 5.

THE LAW OF SIMPLICITY

First things first. How on earth do you get *your* message through? There's so much competing noise already distracting your prospect in such a cluttered world. How do you rise above the daily ruckus, not just the static coming from other advertisers, but the clamorous information explosion we're all living in? (For example, did you know that there is now twice as much new information bombarding us as there was three years ago? Researchers conclude that the amount of new information produced last year alone was about 23 exabytes; an exabyte is one million terabytes; a terabyte is one million megabytes — roughly the contents of one million books as thick as this one.)

We're not the only ones suffering however. Dedicated bird watchers have noted that the Great Tit (Parus major) has had a similar problem. It too has had to find an answer to survive such a noisy place. The clever tit's solution has been to change its song in order to be heard by its potential mates over the loud, low, and continuous racket of the cars, planes and machinery that clutter the soundtrack of modern urban life. Simply put, the bird now sings higher notes when it's near noisy, rumbling main roads and intersections.

Nature understands that in a cluttered world, you must find a way to get yourself into clear space if you're going to communicate successfully. The question is: how do you get your ad into clear space? *Un-clutter.* If you want to be noticed in a jumbled world, be ruthlessly simple. Simplicity is the only foolproof advertising technique. Because it is the only *clutter cutter* that never comes at the cost of comprehension. Indeed, the original lateral thinker, Edward De Bono, believes that simplicity is so valuable in today's business world that he has called for an Institute of Simplicity to be established.

Advertising is communication, and if the right person does not really hear your ad, having heard, does not clearly understand what you are saying, then you've failed. Put starkly, we're living in the over-information age; this means the more information you put into your advertising, the less people will take out. The Law of Simplicity exists to curb the Crime of Add-vertising. Remember, even though it's called an "ad," the most effective way to communicate a message is actually to *subtract* secondary information.

All great messages are profoundly simple: Don't walk; Just do it; I love you; Thou shalt not kill. The enduring philosophical tool, Ockham's Razor, states that when there are two correct answers which solve a problem equally well, the *more* correct answer is the simpler one. Work for a compression of a persuasive idea into a hard nut core — a profound simplicity; a haiku-like intensity.

Ah, but "how difficult it is to be simple," as Van Gogh said. The art, of course, is not how short you make it. But, rather, how to make it short. For Marcello Serpa, the Brazilian advertising superstar and a former chairman of judges at Cannes, simplicity has never been an option for successful advertising. It is the only starting point. The proof is in his work, year after staggeringly successful year: simply stunning. A real high note, as it were, in today's advertising.

THE LAW OF SIMPLICITY BY MARCELLO SERPA

It is much easier to be complex than to be simple. Simplicity is one of the most definite characteristics in advertising and maybe one of the most forgotten. This may be due to the fact that the "simple" has a dual personality: what is simple may have a genius synthesis or simply a primary obviousness.

To be simple requires much more self-confidence than to be complex. The simple may be embarrassing. After all, each of us wants to be seen as a person with refined thoughts. Complexity of rationale may be easily confused with intelligence by the incautious. Meeting rooms around the world are packed with people who, to justify their salaries, issue super-complex opinions regarding the simplest of subjects. Complicating what is simple seems to be a good career stimulator.

Nevertheless, the simple is only sophisticated, only valued, when it is discovered before it becomes obvious. Until it is discovered, is somewhere, close by, but very well disguised. It is necessary for someone to think about it first, to discover it first so that someone else could then say, "Wow, why didn't I think of that before?" Only after this phrase, repeated by many people, is a simple idea transformed into something obvious. I imagine that it must have been something like this with the wheel, the paper clip, the headline "Think small" for VW or the picture of a piece of purple cut silk for the cigarette Silk Cut. Whoever discovers the obvious first becomes a genius, and those who only repeat it remain mediocre.

Think small.

Being simple is also having an objective and trying to reach it with minimum resources, getting there by the shortest route, with minimum energy. In this

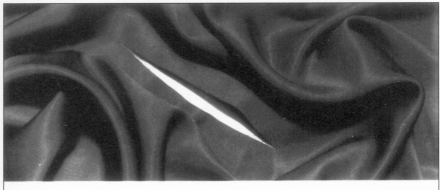

LOW TAR As defined by H.M.Government DANGER Government Health WARNING: CIGARETTES CAN SERIOUSLY DAMAGE YOUR HEALTH

search, everything that does not contribute to simplicity, its purity, must be removed.

Being simple is communicating a new idea using the least possible number of elements, creating something so strong and powerful in its simplicity that it ends up generating a fabulous reaction in whoever is exposed to it. What is simple moves people. It is the revelation, almost sacred, of the obvious: "Gee, why didn't I think of that before?"

Advertising is communication. The result of advertising is measured not by what is said, but by what people understand. A campaign starts to work when whatever is being sold — it may be an institutional message, a promotional price, or a new car — is noticed by those who are exposed to it. But simply being aware that there is a new car in the market is not enough. It is necessary to notice what makes this car different from the others, why it is better. But even this is not enough. It is necessary for this difference to be truly relevant for those who are looking for a car.

It's simple really. You just have to answer two questions: "What am I going to say about this product?" and "Is what I am going to say, truly what is going to motivate people?" The answers to these two questions are the most important part of the creative process for any campaign, TV film or press ad.

Being simple is also being objective before creating.

The capacity of understanding a message depends on each country's social development. A European country, such as England, for example, is used to a level of complexity directly related to its social development. The more complex the society, the higher its capacity of abstraction of more elaborate messages.

In countries such as Brazil, young and still under development, this capacity is much smaller. Being simple and objective is not an option, it is a necessity. Many of the most brilliant English campaigns I know would not have the slightest chance of working in Brazil for being simply unintelligible.

Here, in Brazil, the benefit of a product must be communicated in a clear, straightforward manner so that it may be wholly understood by the greatest number of people.

However, being simple is not enough.

One must be simple and surprising.

Shake the spectator from the lethargy that a commercial break stirs up in people. Make your ad stand out in a magazine that's filled with clichés and artificial images, by smiling and offering itself to whoever reads it, dilating the pupils of its target audience, and thereby conveying its message with the greatest ease.

This is perhaps one of the keys to Brazilian advertising: simple without being simple-minded; objective, yet creating an impact at the same time; popular without being mediocre.

Advertisements such as Guaraná Antarctica, with a minimum of elements, communicate the synthesis of a benefit: No calories, no belly.

Winning the print media Grand Prix at the 1993 Cannes Festival, the ad opened a path that has been followed by many Brazilian agencies since.

Another example of simplicity is the advertisement that announces the Botero exposition at the São Paulo Modern Art Museum (Masp). It defines, with humour, the most striking characteristic of this Colombian artist, who only portrays enormous and obese characters.

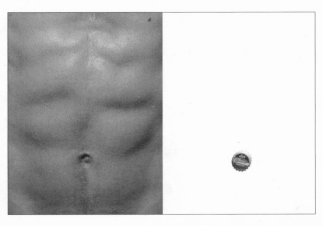

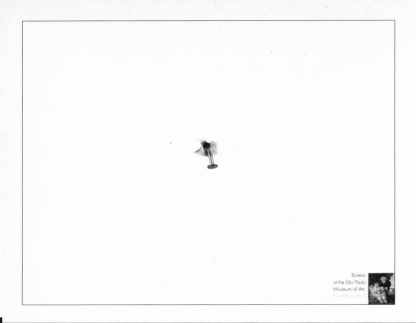

Sparing joints and articulations is one of the most important benefits of a tennis shoe for those who run every day. The Mizuno brand is acknowledged by the Brazilian Orthopedic Society as having the most efficient impact-absorption system in the market. Therefore, imagining a tennis shoe between bones seems to be the simplest solution for the ad.

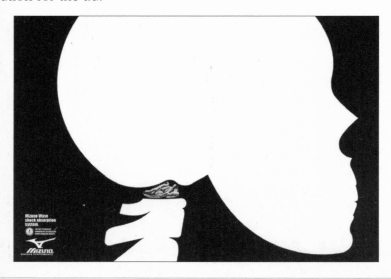

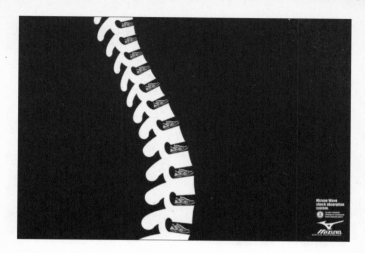

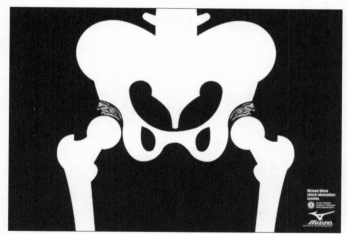

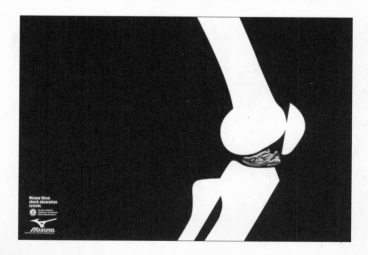

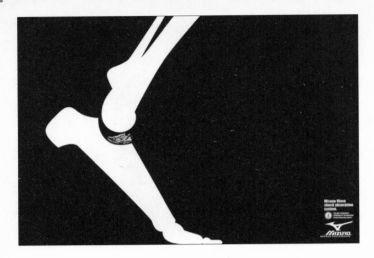

That is how it was with VW as well. Discovering a double check and using it to reinforce the German brand's commitment to the total quality of its products seemed extremely obvious to us.

Jean Marie Dru, then president of the Cannes Festival, commented on some of our pieces that had won several Lions. "Many creative directors in France would never approve them. They are too simple. The French prefer complexity."

I am an enthusiast of what is simple, of the search for the hidden obvious, of the Japanese *Hai Kai*, of the exercise of reduction, of the capacity for the synthesis that Picasso had towards the end of his life.

In answer to someone who criticizes that it was very easy to draw one of his bulls with a trace, he simply said: "I took 50 years to do it."

THE LAW OF POSITIONING

"Positioning" must be among the most repeated words in the advertising lexicon, rivalled only by "research," "morph" and "it wasn't my fault."

What's most remarkable is that marketing survived so long before Al Ries and Jack Trout coined the term and explained their concept. But once they did, everything changed. If they'd patented the word, they'd be rich as Bill Gates. Since then, an understanding of good positioning has made many people wealthy. It's not a panacea, but it is indispensable.

Positioning solves the dangerous Crime of Being in the Wrong Place at the Right Time. Developed to find ways of finding room for new products in highly developed markets, positioning became a major educative concept in the world's developing markets.

Much has changed in the world of marketing since the concept was first aired, and no one is better placed than Al Ries himself to explore how positioning has evolved, and how savvy marketers have become in using it to carve out the richest territory.

THE LAW OF POSITIONING BY AL RIES

Most days, the best-selling advertising book at Amazon.com is *Positioning: The Battle for Your Mind* by Jack Trout and yours truly. What's surprising about this is that the book was published 22 years ago.

For more than two decades, positioning has been a hot topic in the advertising community, and not always favourably. Bill Bernbach wrote an article denouncing the positioning concept and David Ogilvy said, "Phooey on positioning." What is positioning and why does it generate such a love/hate relationship?

The positioning concept challenges an idea that is the heart and soul of the advertising community: that the primary function of advertising is to communicate. "Tell more, sell more" was the old advertising adage.

Advertising as a form of communications is an idea deeply embedded in the corporate psyche. Many advertising departments are now calling themselves the "Marketing Communications Department" or "Marcom" for short. Too bad. The name encourages advertising people to go in exactly the wrong direction.

Advertising is not communications; advertising is positioning. The best advertising communicates little about the product or service. What the best advertising does, however, is to establish and reinforce a position in the prospect's mind.

A little history might be in order. Positioning got its start in 1972 when Jack and I wrote a series of articles entitled "The Positioning Era Cometh" for *Advertising Age* magazine. The series was phenomenally successful. *Advertising Age* sold more than 5,000 reprints of the articles and we printed and gave away 150,000 copies.

As a result of the publicity, we were invited to make hundreds of speeches on the subject (at last count, more than 1,000). We also wrote many dozens of magazine and newspaper articles. In the process, positioning got famous; but somewhere over the last 31 years, the basic idea behind the concept got lost.

Marketing people used to talk about the 4Ps: product, price, place, and promotion. Now they talk about the 5Ps, the original four plus positioning. And no company could launch a new brand without first writing a positioning statement.

When you study these positioning statements, you can see where marketing people have gotten off-track. In general, they are written from the company's point of view: "We want to position our brand as the premier product in the category." What's wrong with a positioning statement like this? Everything. It leaves the prospect out of the equation.

"Positioning is not what you do to the product. Positioning is what you do to the mind of the prospect." This quote from our 1981 book sums up the concept. A positioning statement should be formulated from the prospect's point of view: "There's an open hole in the mind for a premium product in the category. That's the position we want our brand to fill." A semantic game? Maybe. But the truth is, the positioning strategies of most brands utterly fail to take into account the positioning possibilities that might exist in the mind. Let's take a look at some of those possibilities.

The Open Hole

Price is the easiest hole in the mind to understand and it's one of the easiest holes to fill.

Häagen-Dazs' decision to introduce a more expensive line of ice cream set up the "premium" ice-cream position for the brand and made Häagen-Dazs one of the enduring marketing successes of the past several decades.

What Häagen-Dazs did in ice cream, Heineken did in beer. It was the first brand to occupy the high-priced beer position in the mind. Then the folks at Anheuser-Busch decided that if Heineken was the first high-priced *imported* beer, then they could occupy the position as the first high-priced *domestic* beer, a position that the Anheuser-Busch Michelob brand occupies today.

Rembrandt in toothpaste, Evian in water, Orville Redenbacher in popcorn, Rolex in watches, Mercedes-Benz in automobiles: these and hundreds of other brands owe their success to being the first brand to occupy the high-price position in the mind.

High price is only one of the open holes in the mind. Low price is another. What Häagen-Daz, Heineken and Mercedes did at the high end, brands like Wal-Mart and Southwest Airlines have done at the low end.

Minds can change. Stolichnaya was the first vodka to occupy the high-priced position in the mind. As time went on and the Cold War heated up, Americans were turned off by a Russian vodka like Stolichnaya. So Absolut moved smartly into the high-priced vodka position. Today, Absolut outsells Stolichnaya in the US by about three to one.

How many price holes are there in a typical mind? It depends on the category. Normally there are three. The regular brand, the low-priced brand, and the high-priced brand. When you own three brands that occupy all three positions, you can be said to win the Triple Crown of Branding. Anheuser-Busch, for example, has Busch, the largest-selling, low-priced beer; Budweiser, the largest-selling regular beer; and Michelob, the largest-selling high-priced beer.

In some categories, there is room for an "ultra high-priced" brand. Today, Grey Goose vodka, for example, is growing faster than Absolut and is not far behind Stolichnaya in sales, and is sure to pass the Russian brand sometime in the future.

"Country of origin" is another obvious hole in the mind. Toyota was the first to fill the Japanese imported-car hole and became the leading brand. They did it again with Lexus, which became the leading high-priced Japanese automobile brand.

Corona was the first to occupy the Mexican hole in the beer drinker's mind. Beck's was the first to occupy the German hole.

Some consultants have called this positioning strategy, "the first-mover advantage," but that is not so. It's an advantage, but it's not the reason that most leader brands got to be leaders.

It's the "first minder" advantage. That is, the brand that gets into the mind first is the winner, not necessarily the brand that is first in the category.

- Duryea was the first automobile on the road, but never got into the mind. Ford was the first automobile in the mind.
- MITS Altair 8800 was the first personal computer, but never got into the mind. Apple was the first personal computer to get into the mind.
- Du Mont made the first television set; Hurley, the first washing machine. But these and many other brands failed to get into the minds of their prospects. You don't win in the marketplace. You win in the mind.

The New Category

Sometimes there are no open holes in the prospect's mind and you have to create one. We call this positioning strategy: "create a new category you can be first in."

Gatorade, for example, was the first sports drink. Developed in the 1960s by a team of doctors to aid the Gators' football team at the University of Florida, the brand now does over $2 billion in worldwide sales.

PowerBar was the first energy bar and now dominates this fast-growing market. Some critics, of course, think this is just wordplay. PowerBar to them is just a candy bar with a different name to help consumers assuage their guilt feelings about eating a candy bar. Maybe there is little actual difference between a candy bar and a PowerBar, but not so in the mind. Consumers consider them to be two different categories.

Red Bull was the first energy drink. Introduced in Austria in 1987, Red Bull now does more than $1 billion in worldwide sales.

Zima was the first . . . well, what was Zima the first of? The label said "ClearMalt", but nobody knew what that meant. The television announcement ads were no help either. "What's in it?" asked a bartender. "It's a secret. It's something different," replied a mysterious pitchman in his white suit and black hat.

Zima failed to establish a new category and sales remain disappointing. When you want to create a new category and then fill that hole, you need to focus your efforts on selling the category, not the brand.

What's a computer spreadsheet? Almost no one knew what a spreadsheet was until Visi-Calc introduced the first spreadsheet for personal computers such as the 8-bit Apple machines. And then they sold the benefits of the new spreadsheet category. Lotus 1-2-3 was the first spreadsheet for 16-bit machines like the IBM PC. And Microsoft's Excel was the first spreadsheet for the company's Windows operating system. Digital Equipment was the first minicomputer. Dell was the first personal computer sold direct to consumers. Palm was the first handheld computer. Michelin was the first steel-belted, radial-ply tire. Prince was the first oversized tennis racket. And the Callaway Big Bertha was the first oversized golf driver.

These and many other brands became enormous successes by "creating a new category they could be first in."

The Number-two Brand

Consumers like choice. Sometimes you can build a powerful brand just by giving consumers an alternative to the leading brand.

But what strategy can best deliver the number-two position? "Maybe if we can produce a better product than the leader," goes the thinking, "we won't necessarily overtake them, but we will wind up in the number-two position." This is the worst possible approach for a prospective number-two brand. Why? Because the better product cannot win in the marketplace even if consumers expect it to win.

As a matter of fact, there is a strong axiom, or belief, in the minds of consumers that "the best product or service wins in the marketplace." After all, this is so logical and so obvious, who could possibly disagree?

I could, that's who. There's a paradox in marketing. While everyone believes that the better product will win in the marketplace, the worst possible strategy for any company is to try to produce a "better product."

Why is this so? Because the leader in your field has already created the perception of producing the better product. If you try to claim that your product is better, the prospect thinks, "No, it can't be better; otherwise it would be the leader."

Yet what do most companies try to do? They try to (1) produce a better product and (2) communicate that difference to customers and prospects. While it's easy to do (1), it's almost impossible to do (2).

Is Royal Crown cola a better tasting cola than Coca-Cola? Royal Crown thinks so and their research shows that 57% of prospects prefer the taste of Royal Crown cola to Coca-Cola Classic. That's a pretty big difference.

Yet, the better tasting cola (Royal Crown) has only 2% of the cola market. What they need to do, you might be thinking, is to communicate that difference. Well, they've tried that and it doesn't work.

"That can't be," the prospect thinks. "If Royal Crown were the better-tasting cola, it would be the leader, not Coke. There must be something wrong with the research."

Actually, the Royal Crown company hired an independent research organisation to conduct one million taste tests comparing its product with Coca-Cola. Would 10 million taste tests have made a difference? No. You believe what you want to believe and if you believe that the better product wins in the marketplace, then you think Coca-Cola must be the better product because it is the leader.

Then how do you become a strong number-two brand? You become the opposite of the leader. Coca-Cola is the old, established brand which means that your parents drank Coca-Cola. So Pepsi-Cola said, "You don't want to drink what your parents drank, you're the Pepsi Generation."

Listerine was the "bad-tasting" mouthwash that killed germs and odor in your mouth. So Scope became the "good-tasting" mouthwash and a strong number-two brand.

Home Depot is the leading "home-improvement" store, but its crowded aisles and jammed shelves appeal more to men than women. So Loew's became the home-improvement store for women, with its clean layouts and wide aisles.

Windows is the computer operating system you buy from Microsoft. Linux, the fastest-growing computer operating system, is "open source software," or free.

Duality is a fundamental characteristic of a human mind. Say "black" and people also think "white." Say "men" and people also think "women." Say "large" and people also think "small."

Your best chance of occupying that number-two position is to try to become the opposite of the leader. In every category, the mind has an open hole for a number-two brand, just waiting for someone to occupy it.

The Specialist

Every coffee shop in America sells coffee, but they also sell hamburgers, hot dogs, French fries, apple pie, doughnuts, and dozens of other foods and beverages.

So Starbucks specialised in coffee and became a very successful brand. So did McDonald's, which specialised in hamburgers. And Dunkin' Donuts which specialised in doughnuts. And Subway which specialised in submarine sandwiches.

The largest air-cargo company in America was Emery Air Freight. What kind of services did Emery offer? Everything — large packages, small packages, overnight delivery, inexpensive two- and three-day deliveries. So Federal Express specialised in "small packages, overnight" and became a much more successful brand than Emery.

Enterprise Rent-A-Car specialised in the "insurance replacement" business and became the largest car-rental company in America. (If your car is stolen or wrecked and you have an insurance policy to cover it, you are eligible for a free rental car for a period of time.)

In mature categories (such as automobiles) where most of the segments have well-established brands, the best way of positioning your brand is by emphasising a single attribute. Volvo did it with "safety." And BMW did it with "driving." In essence, they each became a specialist in the safety and driving categories.

It's almost always possible to build a brand by occupying a specialist position inside consumers' minds. The only real question is, "is the category going to be big enough?"

Left-handed golf clubs might be a specialist position, but perhaps it's not a big enough market for a brand to exploit.

The Channel Brand

Hanes was the largest-selling panty-hose brand in department stores in America, but Hanes had a problem. Women were not shopping at department stores frequently enough. So the company wanted to expand its distribution.

Supermarkets were the logical choice. (Women visit a supermarket almost twice a week.) So Hanes developed a second brand for supermarket distribution only. The "L'eggs" name was a particularly good choice because it was a double entendre (legs and eggs). To reinforce the name, the product was packaged in a plastic container that looked like an egg. L'eggs, the first supermarket panty-hose brand, became the largest-selling panty-hose brand in the country.

The Internet has created many opportunities to create channel brands. Amazon.com, eBay, Monster.com, Salesforce.com are just some of many successful "Internet-only" brands.

Paul Mitchell has become a $600 million hair and skin-care brand by focusing on the professional hair-salon channel. Ping did the same with golf clubs by focusing on the pro-shop channel. Amway did the same by focusing on the MLM (multi-level marketing) channel.

One of the most under-used methods of building a brand is the "channel" brand. As new channels are introduced, they create many opportunities to do just that.

The Gender Brand

Sometimes you can build a brand by focusing on half the market.

- Marlboro became a big brand by positioning itself as the first cigarette for men.
- Virginia Slims became a big brand by positioning itself as the first cigarette for women.
- Right Guard became a big brand by positioning itself as the first deodorant for men.
- Secret became a big brand by positioning itself as the first deodorant for women.

The "Bad Name" Problem

Complicating the search for an open hole in the mind is the issue of the name. You can't put a square peg in a round hole and you can't fill a hole in the mind with a bad, or inappropriate, name.

Ralph Lifshitz was a young fashion designer in New York who aspired to better things. So he changed his name to Ralph Lauren and made his Polo brand into the most successful fashion brand in the world. Could he have accomplished his goal with the name Polo Ralph Lifshitz? Of course not.

Marion Morrison wanted to become a cowboy movie star so he changed his name to John Wayne and became the most successful motion-picture star ever. Could he have accomplished his goal with the name Marion? Of course not.

Many Asian names will not work outside of Asia. Names like Daewoo, Daihatsu and Matsushita are difficult to pronounce and difficult to spell outside of Asia. When the Tokyo Tsushin Kogyo company started to market its products in the US, the company changed its name to Sony. A good move. Many Asian companies that want to establish worldwide brands will have to do the same.

The "One Name, Two Holes" Problem

Then there is the problem of trying to use the same name to fill two different holes. Xerox, the leading brand of office copier, tried to get into the mainframe computer market with the Xerox name. It was a disaster.

IBM, the leading brand of mainframe computers, tried to get into the personal computer market with the IBM name. The company has lost hundreds of millions of dollars trying to fill two holes with one name.

Are there successful examples of line extension? Sure, but these generally happen in weak markets where no single brand dominates the category. Or they happen with weak brands with little identity in their categories. (In other words, if your brand doesn't stand for anything in one category, you can move it to another category where it won't stand for anything either.)

But when brands have a strong position in the mind, they can't be moved. Could Coca-Cola beer successfully challenge Budweiser? Silly question.

The "Moving-the-Hole" Problem

Some companies think they can change what their brands stand for. So Volkswagen is trying to sell a $100,000 automobile called the Phaeton. And Mercedes-Benz is trying to sell $20,000 A-class vehicles. Both endeavors are unlikely to be successful in the long run.

You can deepen a hole, you can broaden a hole, but the one thing you can't do with a hole is move it. When a brand is strongly established in the mind, it can rarely, if ever, be moved to a new location.

There's a lot more to say about positioning. We've only scratched the surface of the subject in this chapter. (Interested readers might want to obtain a copy of the 20th Anniversary Edition of *Positioning*, with added illustrations and comments by Jack and myself.)

You can't go wrong, however, if you take your mind off your product, your brand, and your company and focus instead on the mind of the consumer.

That's where you can win and that's where you can also lose.

THE LAW OF CONSISTENCY

The Law of Consistency has a natural-born enemy. The Crime of the New Broom. A change in the marketing department usually ushers in sweeping changes to agency, campaign and brand direction. Problem is, the public often tires of a campaign at a much slower rate than marketing executives. The history of advertising is littered with abandoned campaigns, like unfashionable spouses, that have been replaced with new models long before the original has worn out.

Or, sometimes, even worn in.

Consumers frequently remember a brand's campaign long after everyone in the company's organisation has forgotten the name of the idiot client who canned it in the first place.

New agencies, and new creative directors, are just as guilty as client executives of this impatient sin. Many are eager to make their own mark, often at the expense of the carefully constructed thinking and positioning of the originators.

Consistency, like simplicity, is an uphill battle in the dynamic, change-worshipping culture of advertising.

After all, the setting up and solving of new issues is what fuels the momentum of the marketing process. The task of remaining consistent is made harder these days with the number of multimedia touch points a campaign must maintain with consumers, along with the increasing number of hands guiding it through these various permutations and extensions.

In 2003, Heinz in the UK announced, to the horror of nostalgic consumers, that it was taking a "long hard look" at its 36-year-old slogan, Beanz Meanz Heinz. The widely-loved catchphrase that had already survived an attempt on its life a decade earlier, when agency BMP ran with Heinz Builds Britz. However, the original recipe for success stood the test of time and was reinstated within three years.

Another example: Toyota in the US dropped their "Oh What a Feeling" campaign within a couple of years of it being devised in the late 1970s. Yet the notion lived on in other markets, like Australia, where it became the best-known slogan in any advertising category, as well as the most creatively awarded campaign, in the country.

Meanwhile, the US Toyota client was spending tens of millions of dollars trying to embed a different tagline, then another, and another, without capturing the burr-like quality of the original. Or ever matching the creative firepower of the Antipodean work. In the name of efficacy, they swallowed some pride and at last returned to the gist of it (Get the Feeling) in 2001.

There are several global blue chip advertisers who could learn from Toyota's percipience. A number of techniques can make consistency easier to achieve, like the creative use of brand properties, mnemonic devices, and demonstrably campaignable ideas, for a start.

An advertising property is like a house; maintain it, freshen it up every couple of years, and it will last a lifetime.

In his book, *Asian Branding*, Ian Batey, founder of the Southeast Asian powerhouse agency, Batey

Ads, argued passionately for campaign consistency. His agency's long-running Singapore Girl campaign, for Singapore Airlines (SIA), set all kinds of benchmarks for advertising in the region, and is a model example of steady and successful brand building.

Consistency, he says, is the only way to fly.

The Law of Consistency by Ian Batey

In the East, the trader mentality still prevails: buy and sell, buy and sell. It is tough to accept a formula that suggests one should build anything like brand equity for the long term. When Asian brands look to global markets, a completely different mindset is needed.

One upside of thinking short is being able to move fast; and that is the bottom-line attraction for the Asian investor. However, in the marketing arena, expediency often devalues brands in a flash.

Clearly, the advertising communications services industry in Asia has been delinquent. Our industry simply hasn't yet got its act together in educating Asian brand owners on the great upsides of developing positive brand strategies and long-term brand building. Our industry, too, has allowed itself to be distracted by short-term thinking and practices.

The ways of the West have reached into the heart and soul of Asia, and teenagers — the big Asian consumers of tomorrow — are relishing and embracing it all. And why not!

In the face of this, the main thing is to retain one's core values. Yet no marketing model should be so rigid that you can't finesse it. No corporate marketing mantra can be so rigid that any change, any flexibility, is *verboten*.

Corporately, one can say: "Here's the model we've always used; so let's see if it works in a particular society."

For instance, Marlboro has never significantly changed its platform since the 1970s, whether it's talking to men who dig ditches or the men who sit in boardrooms. The brand touches everyone in the same way. But when they get into each individual marketplace, the Marlboro team may have to be very flexible because each market has its own rules and regulations.

Strategic guidelines would not change; *tactical* ones would.

Global consistency in its advertising has been the cornerstone of Marlboro's power. Because it is visually very strong and simple, everyone can understand it and the values it projects. Marlboro's success among young and old in Asia is a fine example of how a well-established Western brand identity has triumphantly crossed all kinds of cultural and social barriers and has stayed true to itself in the process.

Marketing a global brand that seeks substantial growth across a large group of people should try to follow much the same model anywhere. It's just plain common sense. This fast-shrinking world of communications and the fast-growing movement of people across continents are two reasons for consistency.

Another is the need for a consistent brand soul to present to all people.

The brand-bonding mission is a tough one. Businessmen in Asia are not renowned risk-takers in an esoteric area like marketing. They are conspicuous for their conservative approach. However, underneath the surface lies an energy that loves to take financial risks at the race track and casinos, so we — the communications services industry — have to find more creative ways to get Asian brand owners to commit to more courageous brand-building programs.

My sense is that a brand's soul could start to lose its way if the diverse creative expressions across the globe are allowed to move further away from the brand's core values. I'm definitely in favor of central control of global brands and I think most brand owners would support this view. However, you need regular checks and balances to make sure you're scoring well.

The marketer of an everyday product — toothpaste, detergent, a product that is aiming for the masses, the people in public housing or out in the villages — must take into account the local culture, the local viewpoint. Nonetheless, the central architecture on which the brand was built need not change.

The success of Marlboro — the Marlboro cowboy has become an international icon in countries where cowboys never existed — reinforces the power of consistently promoting one's core branding properties. Wherever legally possible, their brand advertising is universally the same all over the world, pitched to every socio-economic level.

Levi's provides another fine example of great global brand building from the centre. All young people share much the same universal traits, grappling with authority and coming to terms with their place in society. By concentrating its advertising on the similarities, Levi's overcomes the differences.

What is Consistency?

Lifetime bonding is the ultimate dream of all ambitious brand owners. People love to be loved and, predictably, they gravitate towards brands that know them, understand them and reach into their hearts.

For this, consistency — a single message — must be maintained across time, geography, media product and ad channels.

Brand Equity

Although only formalised as a concept about 20 years ago, brand equity is by far the most valuable asset of most companies. It has been described as "the upstream reservoir of cash flow"; consumer motivation to buy or to pay more has taken place, but it hasn't yet been translated into actual sales turnover. The very fact that brand equity is intangible makes the job of protecting and enhancing it that much harder.

Being true to the brand begins by ensuring that the brand owner's staff, distributors, partners and agents understand the brand's identity. They should have a good grip on what the brand stands for: what is timeless about it and what is not. Any genuine global brand-building effort should include programs that educate employees. Everyone must know and enthusiastically support what aspects of brand strategy have to be followed like Moses's Commandments and which ones can be varied to meet local needs. If the brand owner's own staff don't understand and embrace what he is trying to build, what chance has the public got?

Global brands are naturally obliged to transcend borders; sometimes those borders are jealously guarded within the company itself. More seminars, workshops, field visits and work-exchange programs will knock down walls. Cross-border bonding not only nurtures a freer flow of information and co-operation, it also lets a company develop its own marketing vocabulary and templates. Systems can also be put in place to track when brand-building efforts drift off strategy. Getting employees to vote on the ad campaigns they think best exemplify the essence of the brand builds involvement; more importantly, it signals whether employees fully understand what the brand is all about.

Every brand owner has to find his own way of being true to his brand but whatever model is employed, enthusiastic support of the program at local market level is fundamental. We sometimes forget that the lads and lasses in the territorial trenches are the brand's first line of defence, and attack.

Keeping true to yourself and your brand requires eternal vigilance.

The Danger of Change

While variety is the spice of life, change isn't.

Contrary to popular opinion, I figure that mature consumers generally resist change. On the other hand, many marketers feel change is their salvation. So do advertising agencies. It is conventional to change; it is *un*conventional not to.

The world is changing so fast, or so we're told. Information technology is upon us, changing us. Everything has to change to survive. It's as though we are all racing down a fast-flowing river, jostling each other to lead the race, with little concern or knowledge of where the river is taking us — and it could well be to Niagara Falls.

You don't have to jump blindly into that fast-flowing river.

You don't have to be totally obsessed about change.

Sit back and calmly get the perspectives in balance.

Brands are Made Up of Three Parts:
The Body, the Soul and the Conscience

The body is the change engine; it represents the tangibles of your brand offering, the product developments and enhancements that are an ongoing process.

The brand's soul represents the emotional side of your brand offering; it is usually deep-rooted, and mirrors the unique character, personality and culture of your brand.

The brand's conscience represents the company's corporate "payback" responsibility to specific target customers or to the public at large. If large consumer marketers are serious about global growth for their brand, the three dynamics must come into play.

The mission of the brand body is pretty clear — it is your engine of regular upgrades and innovations. Where things frequently go off the rails for marketers and ad agencies alike is the handling of the brand's soul. They apply consistent change to the look, the feel, the personality and the underlying compelling core appeal of the brand. This is like getting Frank Sinatra to sing like Elvis Presley, and *then* like Pavarotti, just to be trendy.

Getting the brand's soul right is not an easy task, but once you've nailed it, it need not essentially change for decades. The brand's soul is the mother of the brand, and like a country's national flag and anthem, it should have a positive, long-term place in consumers' hearts. After consumers get the teenage adrenaline out of their system, they are not keen on constant cosmetic change.

The brand's conscience has been an integral part of the game among big global brand owners for generations. As it is more "corporate citizen" and institutional in character, it should tend to reflect the values of the brand's soul and not be the target of constant change.

As the 21st century takes off, this part of the brand's composition will expand in size and commercial value. Asian brand owners (most of whom are not yet embracing this development) should take note to address this responsibility more seriously from now on if they have global ambitions.

A colleague contends that while a great brand is "the property of the world," it is "subtly different to every individual. There is, however, an essential core in a brand that strikes a universal resonance and that becomes the lowest common denominator — or the highest common factor — across the brand."

While I think my colleague struck the right nerve on certain points, his view complicates the issues of brand building and "change". If the people who talk the change game are a bit difficult to understand, what chance have others, especially brand owners, in coming to grips with the issue?

Vigilance is the key watchword.

Remember what the Singapore Girl is. She is the warm, gentle, caring personality in her *sarong kebaya* forever and ever. What, however, does change is that she consistently offers you better on-line booking systems, wider seats, wider, aisles, more cocktails, better food, more sophisticated in-flight entertainment, and so on. It is equally essential to ensure that the Singapore Girl retains youthfulness and freshness as the years turn into decades.

We therefore endeavour to consistently *contemporise the advertising through the story compositions and the production values* — the structure of the content, the styling of the film, the soundtrack, the still photography. Execution can play a big role in shaping a brand's distinctive identity.

It's a recipe that aims to always keep the Singapore Girl relevant and uniquely appealing to consumers.

Brand building is like building a relationship with a friend. If you connect fairly regularly, you stand a good chance of nurturing the friendship. If for some reason he or she declines to a chat once every six months, then once a year, or maybe you may see each other every two years, you'll gradually forget each other.

It's the same thing in advertising. If you're serious, you've got to keep up a regular dialogue; you've got to keep nurturing the relationship. You've got to get your customers interested in you, bonded to you.

Even when times are tough, and business is slow, somehow you've got to sustain a level of contact that signals your genuine desire to retain a relationship with your customers. If you cut off the connection over an extended period, the downside could be extremely dark and life-threatening for your brand.

A global brand I admire is Rolex. Over the years, it has gradually moved from being a well-known, admired brand into what all brands aspire to

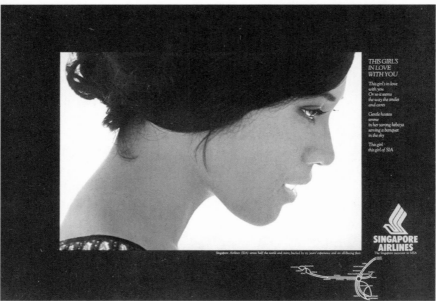

The ad that launched the icon. The phrase Singapore Girl came later, making its appearance in the lyrics of the song. The brand proposition has been delivered consistently for 30 years.

be — an institution. Rolex has invested 30 to 40 years of consistent brand-building in order to institutionalise its brand.

It hasn't changed its core brand platform in all that time.

Even when the economy is tough, its advertising program is relentless. It communicates six-star quality and has always had a strong endorsement program: great intellectual achievers, great explorers, great singers, and always the more lofty names. Some people say the ads are unexciting and unchanging, but I think their strength has been their unchanging, focused view of the way life should be.

Just keeping up basic connection is an art in itself. Whenever you put your company name or trademark in a communication you are conveying a brand message; you are doing brand advertising. So *all* ads are brand ads, which means a commitment to upholding the brand's values across everything.

Propositions can vary. The media can vary. But the brand's voice should be "family." As far as the consumer is concerned, every piece of communication they see is a brand ad. There is no such thing as having A-grade ads, B-grade ads and C-grade ads.

The same people, charged with building the brand, should approve every ad. Once you adopt this thinking, you'll find that your marketplace presence will become distinctly sharper.

A Unique Icon Or Property

Its unlikely that the Marlboro Man will be bettered as a visual icon, although some of the world's most successful campaigns have not had a graphic icon in their communications.

I just happen to believe that a compelling, exclusive graphic entity is a huge asset in this game and that this ingredient should be firmly on the agenda in developing new brand-communications programs.

Apart from graphic characters, there are numerous other properties that can be employed exclusively to the brand's advantage. A unique wordsmith style is one; the quintessential slogan is another. Then there are catchphrases that potentially become part of everyday language, or squeeze more life out of the trademark symbol like Nike has done.

Creating and massaging exclusive brand icons or properties is an essential prerequisite in a brand-building exercise.

Brand builders must be firm and focused. *There are no half measures building a brand.* If an ad isn't right, if the language is wrong, if it is not the brand talking, say so. *Every ad should be making a small investment in the brand's eternal worth.*

Success has its challenges. One you become a global brand leader in both profits and reputation, there is a tendency to move to a defensive strategy, to protect your treasure, to look for safeguards rather than retain the adventurous spirit that won you fame and fortune in the first place.

I have no problem with the argument that different target audiences and different consumer feelings require different advertising solutions. What I do have a problem with is when the only thing that links all the different ads together is the company logo.

Remember, please, that every worthy brand has a soul, a special personality. It is a fundamental responsibility for brand owners to leverage their personality in one form or another in *all* their advertising. It's all part of the brand-building exercise. It's part of consistently connecting in a certain way with your customer. It's the art of putting yourself head and shoulders above the din of characterless advertising.

Life for the global brands will get better and better and the global brand will triumph *so long as the connection with the consumer is seen by the consumer as relevant, genuine and friendly.*

Every brand owner with regional or global aspirations can learn from Mercedes-Benz. Here is the living proof that *great global brands should never be changed to suit one or two markets.* The brand, its values and its voice must never be compromised. Mercedes-Benz is the same car, representing the same excellence, wherever it goes in the world. It is what it is.

Look at the brands that have had consistently good advertising over several years. Now look at the clients behind that advertising. In every case, it will be a strong, prosperous organisation. A focused, dynamic, confident brand owner and his agency generally have a close working relationship in which the agency is encouraged to explore and expand creative boundaries so long as the brand's core values are nourished rather than reinvented.

Strong clients know their own brand disciplines. So do their agencies. They work as one in building the brand's relationship with consumers. Nowadays, unfortunately, this is actually the exception rather than the rule. It is very tough to keep focused. More brand owners are starting to jump around in all directions, championing the need for change. And the process of change to some brand owners means different brand values, different New Age advertising and so on.

In some cases, they may well be correct, but in most, they are not. They are merely confusing themselves.

This is a fine line.

The brand's core values need not change, whereas the creative delivery of those values should constantly be at the cutting edge. Somehow brand owners get that confused; then they confuse their advertising agencies, and their final advertising reflects the lost path and confuses the consumer as well.

If you wish to create a reputation for yourself, whatever you do, branding is the name, branding is the game. Branding has always been the major bugle player in the marketing battle. With the invasion of the Internet, the smart card and other technology, branding is now the Napoleon in the battle.

The brand is no longer just a marketing concept. The brand is now a financial concept; *it is a company's most important financial asset.*

4

THE LAW OF SELLING

"**A**dvertising may be described as the science of arresting human intelligence long enough to get money from it," said Canadian humorist Stephen Leacock.

That's why the techniques in this book — these laws, hints, insights, revelations and instinctual leaps — are not intrinsically valuable. They are here for one purpose.

To sell.

Advertising is a means to an end.

We are here to ring up sales not win gongs. Trouble is, too much advertising has become adept at drawing too much attention to itself for its own sake, without being able to go that final 95% of the distance, closing the deal for the product that is behind the idea.

Critics of much current advertising, for example, accuse it of striving to be too clever. Too smart can be smart arse. Clever for clever's sake.

It is argued by clients that advertising creative people have too many non-commercial preoccupations, like creative awards and funny-shaped, glittering prizes. The desired response most creative people want from their ad is for their peers to say, "Gee, I wish I'd thought of that."

This can lead to The Crime of Circus Performing. The chairman of the first agency I worked in, Eric Maguire, described an analogy with circus artists performing death-defying stunts to impress their peers. The high-wire people become so good at their trade that they are no longer turned on by the applause of the paying customers. Instead, they begin playing to the other circus performers, the only people who have any real understanding of the skill that goes into their act. In the end, they wind up doing things that are unbelievably difficult and dangerous for the benefit of the handful of experts who could understand and admire their accomplishment. Accidents, or even death, are a natural corollary.

Advertising creativity is also a high wire act. The audience that writers and art directors most like to impress is the writers and art directors in other agencies. Perhaps because only that group is capable of recognising how well (or badly) the ad has been done.

I'm not saying any would deliberately torpedo a client's marketing plan in order to do something noticeable but totally irrelevant; however, the simple truth is that, for many, their greatest kicks come not from piling one dollar on top of another, but from the recognition of their skill by other craftsmen.

That's not just a crime, it's a sin.

One of the UK's foremost advertising evangelists, Dave Trott, founder of agency Walsh Trott Chick Smith, has never lost sight of the true goal of advertising, despite the distracting number of creative awards he's been given over the years.

Here, he discusses the Law of Selling and describes the simple binary method he uses to keep his advertising on the job.

Buy into it.

THE LAW OF SELLING BY DAVE TROTT

Can anyone remember the purpose of advertising? Why we get paid to do what we do?

Are we TV sitcom writers, to make people laugh?

Are we gag writers for observational comedians, putting our finger on telling truths?

Are we prose stylists, delivering beautifully written passages of literature?

I'd like to suggest a terribly old-fashioned view of the fundamental purpose of what we do, that I know will get me laughed out of every trendy media bar and restaurant in Soho.

It's the "S" word (gasp!). (What? You mean talking people into buying things, like a shop assistant? Man, where did you go to university?)

Yes, I know we don't do anything as crass as that anymore. Nowadays, we're much more sophisticated: we "build brands."

We don't look at the sales figures, we look at the tracking scores.

Never mind if anyone's buying it, have we not won an IPA Effectiveness Award, or a D&AD pencil?

We don't sell products to consumers anymore. Now we sell OUR product: advertising. And we sell it to our clients and peers: in Soho, Cannes, or Lurzer's Archive. Not only hasn't the Emperor got any clothes, none of the rest of us have either.

I thought we'd reached the zenith (your zenith is my nadir) of this type of non-advertising during the dotcom boom. When computer nerds with fistfuls of cash wandered into agencies and said "make something we like, man," we did — great pieces of film that all the new media types love. Of course we didn't deign to do anything so crude as telling consumers what the product was, or why they should buy it.

So guess what? They didn't.

The dotcom boom was the time people started to believe you just had to "build brand," not sell product. When the dotcoms disappeared, the non-advertising industry built up on their backs stayed around, teaching a new generation of marketing trainees that the "S" word is dinosaur thinking.

What really clever people do is "brand building": brand diamonds, brand keys, brand doughnuts, brand personality, brand profile, brand signature, brand architecture, brand onion, brand halo. Say the word "brand" often enough and everything will be okay.

Now, I'm not saying that building the brand isn't ever the answer. What I am saying is, it isn't always the answer. But it's become a simple knee-jerk solution to avoid the discomfort of thinking about the "S" word.

It has become a religion.

And the purpose of all religions is to avoid thinking, to keep you in a state of belief and superstition. Which is what "brand" has become, the advertising superstition.
Like touching wood.

Of course there are great brands which can charge a premium for any product with their name attached. But (and, like anything that questions religion, this is going to sound like heresy) before they were great brands they were great products.

How the brands got built was that the advertising sold the product in an appropriate way. (The brand building is the part that's underlined.)

And a brand got built.

Now, once a brand's built, you can sell the brand because it exists.

But before the product builds the brand, you can't sell the brand, because it doesn't exist. And it's silly to sell something that doesn't exist, isn't it? So why are so many of us still doing something that's silly?

Well, let's take a look at how religions work.

The truly blessed are those who have faith, those who believe without questioning. But what if you're a little confused about what a "brand" is, and how it works? Well, like any religion, we have priests to guide you in the mysterious ways of "brand," specialists who write articles about what "brand" is, how "brand" works, "brand" beliefs, even mistaken "brand" beliefs. We have seminars, conferences, and books about the different manifestations of "brand".

All agree on one thing, "brand" is totally mysterious to the mind of man, and "brand" is all powerful.

The problem is, if you substitute belief for thinking, you believe your answer is always right in every situation, no matter what.

And, of course, it isn't.

Which is why we have so much expensive advertising failing all the time. One problem with blindly following this route is that, handled lazily, many brand values are the same within a particular market. (How many times have you seen the brand defined as "modern, approachable and honest" on a brief?)

So if all the brands in the market are selling similar brand values, who wins? It's a no-brainer because, unless you change the dynamics of the market, the market leader must win more from any market growth. So, given that there's usually only one brand leader in any market, pure brand advertising is going to be wrong more often than it's right.

But if "brand" advertising isn't infallible, what else is there?

I'd like to suggest thinking for ourselves as an alternative to blind faith. The problem, as we've seen with "brand", is that we have a whole industry of people dedicated to making what we do as complicated as possible, dedicated to making it virtually impenetrable to any outsiders.

We need to demystify the process.

We need to give everyone access to it.

We need a device so simple anyone can use it.

So that the best solution wins, not just the most complicated one.

That's where what I call, the Binary brief comes in.

It's called "binary" because all you do is choose between two alternatives,

FIGURE 1

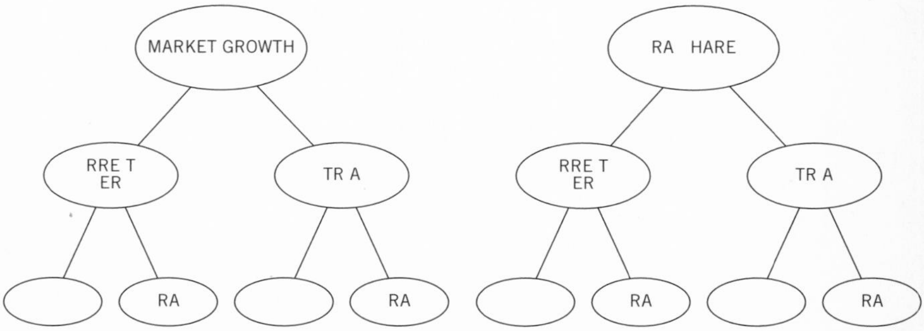

like the zeros and ones of binary code. Like the binary code, it's fast, and it's unambiguous.

But the real value of the process is the rigid discipline that you need to apply to the result.

You must only choose ONE of each pair of alternatives. The questions are ranked in three levels.

(1) What?

(2) Who?

(3) How?

That's it.

(1) What does the advertising need to achieve?
Should we grow the market, and (if we're number one) take the major share of the increase?
Or should we go up against whoever's bigger than us, and try to take a share from them?

(2) Who should we target?
Can we get our current users to buy more of our product, or buy it more often?
Or should we be looking to get people who've never tried it to switch to it?

(3) How do we do it?
Do we have a genuine Unique Selling Propostion (USP)? (A "perceived" USP is fine, but the letter "S" is really important. It's all very well being unique, but does anyone want what we're unique for?)

Or should we be selling the brand?

If so, how?

NOW is when vast army of brand-building specialists can get involved, because now we know what we're doing, who we're doing it to, and why.

This all makes sense, right?

In fact it's so simple it's hardly worth bothering with.

So how come it took the marketing brains at Pepsi-Cola half a century to get to this clarity of thinking?

In fact, just to illustrate how it works, let's hold the two Cola giants against the Binary brief.

FIGURE 2

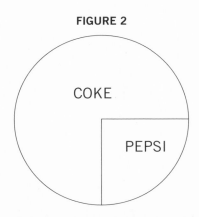

Coca-Cola was obviously number one in the cola market. All they needed to do was sell cola values and they'd get the major share of any growth in the market.

Pepsi looks at Coca-Cola, sees they got successful and thinks: "We'll do the same thing."

You see it in every market.

Numbers two and three are so hypnotised by Number One that they let them make the rules for that market, and are scared to deviate.

"Brand advertising worked so well for Number One, we'd better do the same thing, but with our name on the end." And, because you're in the same market, the brand values you are selling are usually the same brand values that number one is selling.

So the market grows, and Number One takes the major share of that growth, thank you very much.

FIGURE 3

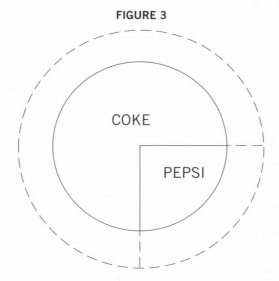

It took Pepsi many decades to wake up and realise that as long as they were selling cola values, they were just doing Coke's advertising for them. They had to start talking people out of Coke and into Pepsi. They had to aggressively go for brand share.

FIGURE 4

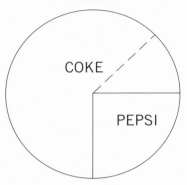

FIGURE 5

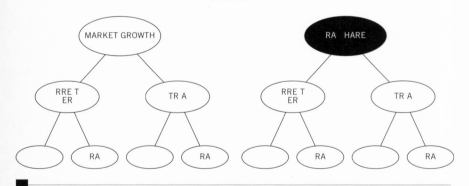

So how to do that?

Well obviously they had to be talking to people about why they should try Pepsi. They had to go for Triallists.

FIGURE 6

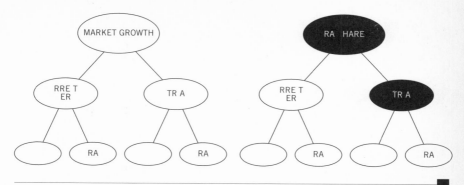

Fair enough, but what message was going to get Coke drinkers to change brands?

Well, selling Pepsi according to cola values hadn't worked. Why would anyone switch from Coke?

They needed something differentiating.

They'd needed a reason.

"Pepsi Tastes Better" is a good place to start, if you can back it up. They had research that could.

So they went for USP: Take the Pepsi challenge.

The aggressive nature of the advertising (selling the product in an appropriate way) became the Pepsi brand. Now they have better advertising than they've ever had, and none of it's for Coke. So, according to the Binary brief, Pepsi went for: Brand Share, Triallists, USP.

FIGURE 7

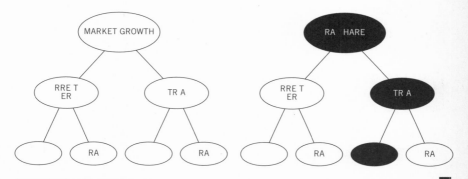

Meanwhile, Coke was more interested in growing the market. They figured they could get much more growth from increasing the overall size of the market than they could from worrying about taking share from their smaller competitor.

FIGURE 8

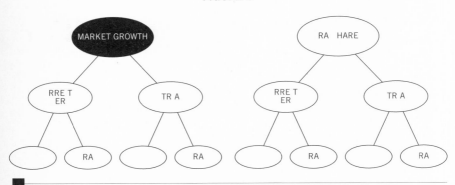

So they kept selling Cola values.

The problem was everyone, everywhere had already tried Coke, so how do you increase sales ? The answer was get existing customers to consume more.

FIGURE 9

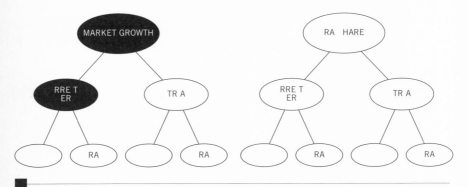

So the message became "Don't just have a Coke on your own, have one with a friend, it's much nicer to share."

"I'd like to buy the world a Coke."

Finally, Coke virtually built the cola market, so it could just appropriate all the market values to itself.

They must do brand advertising.

So, against the binary brief, Coca-Cola went for: market growth, current consumers, brand.

FIGURE 10

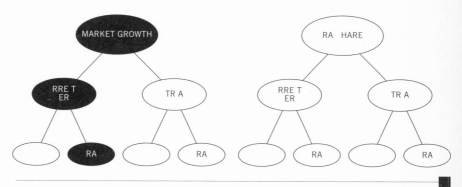

So that's how it works. You make three simple choices and you have one of eight possible advertising strategies.

All your advertising is briefed according to those choices. All your advertising is judged against them.

You can make the decision-making process as complex and thorough as you want, you can take days arguing back and forth over each decision. But at the end, you must have chosen only one of each of the alternatives.

That all sounds simple enough, right?

Well it is simple. But it's not easy.

It's very tough to make those choices. And that's the whole point.

Most marketing people, clients and agencies, live in denial. They want their advertising to include all of those alternatives.

They don't want to leave out anything. They refuse to make those choices. So they get made for them by the consumer.

Remember the old analogy of throwing six tennis balls at the consumer, and they won't catch any?

Well that's not quite true.

Throw six tennis balls at the consumer and they'll probably catch one.

But there's a five in one chance that it won't be the one you wanted them to catch.

So make the decision up front, don't trust to luck. If you're a creative, take a look at the brief you're working on: have they made those choices? If you're a client, take a look at the advertising you're being shown: Is it clear from the ads what those choices are? Because if it isn't clear to you, what possible chance has the consumer got of working it out?

That is, of course, assuming that we're still doing advertising for consumers. And not just as some vague "extension of the PR component of the brand building exercise."

Understand, there's nothing wrong with brand-building.

But only when it's appropriate.

My problem is that, because it's kept so vague and ephemeral, it's used to cover up an awful lot of lazy thinking. That's why I think we need to demystify the whole process.

We don't want ordinary thinking and clever words.

We want clever thinking and ordinary words.

That's why it's time to bring the "S" word out of the closet.

I think we can stop being ashamed of what we do, and pretending we're doing something else. I think the consumers have worked out what those little films between the programmes are for. I think they know they're adverts. They just don't know: who, what or why.

THE LAW OF EMOTION

As far back as the 1990s, world-renowned neuroscientist, AR Damasio, showed that no decision we humans make is based wholly on rational thinking.

Our highly developed neocortex equips us to perform wondrous feats of reason and analysis, but it is still wired up through our older, *emotionally driven*, biological brain.

Which means, no matter how hard we *think* that we have actually thought about a decision, we can't *make* that decision until we interface with our senses, emotions, instinct, and intuition. So, don't let them ever tell you that advertising isn't brain surgery.

In another study, according to the University of Washington: "Brain scan imaging supports the idea that every time you have to make a choice in your personal life, you need to *feel* the projected emotional outcome of each choice — subconsciously or intuitively." You then make that choice according to that projected feeling.

In short, the mind engages its emotional centres even when making decisions as simple as whether to wear a seatbelt or to have cake rather than broccoli. John Kenneth Galbraith knew this years ago when he said: "A person buying ordinary products in a supermarket is in touch with his deepest emotions." Research conducted on supermarket shoppers and published in the *Journal of Marketing* in the 1990s, showed that only 51% could recall the most logical feature of a product they'd just placed in their trolley: the price of the item.

Human beings think with their feelings and emotions. Our instincts reach out and somehow feel what seems good for our souls, or bad.

Human decision-making is emotional, spiritual, political and, perhaps least of all, rational. The truth is, we aren't really rational beings. We are more human than that.

In his *On Equilibrium,* Canadian author John Ralston Saul explains that human action and thought naturally tries to balance six "qualities": common sense, ethics, imagination, intuition, memory and then, lastly, reason.

On average, in a supermarket, this process takes about 12 seconds. And, in 85% of purchases, only the chosen brand is handled.

You reach out for the one you love. I use these wide ranging references to contrast with marketing's ongoing addiction to heartless rationality, which seems to me to be often out of step with the way consumers live their lives. Marketing's reliance on logic and minutely reasoned, feature-filled advertising has created a disconnection between brands and real people. "Management concerns are relatively narrow — relative, that is, to life, knowledge and possibility," wrote Don Watson in *Death Sentence — The Decay of Public Language.*

Client executives often think that emotion is wishy-washy and, worse, rules out hard sell creative. This is not right.

In my book, *Creative Leaps,* I told the story of a street vendor I saw selling flowers one Valentine's

Day. She had a chalk-drawn sign in front of her flower stall that economically, and suggestively, promised: "Flowers today. Fireworks tonight." Her very effective ad didn't describe the details of the flowers' varying features, only their substantial and emotional benefit at the end of the day. This is far more convincing than facts and parity features.

However, selling emotion to clients is a tough business. Marketing, after all, is a process-driven occupation. The UK creative powerhouse, BBH, found a way of building emotion into the process by moving away from the reason-centric, fact-focussed Unique Selling Proposition (USP), to the Emotional Selling Proposition (ESP) and have produced some landmark work throughout the last decade. The ESP allows advertising to more persuasively sell the *idea* of the brand, rather than the mere product itself.

Englishman John Shaw lives in Hong Kong and is Director of Planning for the region at Ogilvy & Mather. Here, he discusses the selling power of emotion around the globe, in the most logical and reasoned way.

THE LAW OF EMOTION BY JOHN SHAW

In 1983, Andrex was lost for words. It led the British toilet tissue market and was one of the most valuable grocery brands in the country. All was not rosy, however. A competitor had come out with a marvellously soft product, a product that people loved when they tried it, a product that delighted the fingers and caressed the posterior. Andrex was vulnerable, and the brand's owners knew it. But Andrex stood to lose a rational argument, hands down.

A look back at the television advertising for Andrex in 1983 and 1984 will show a playful Labrador puppy running joyfully through a series of seasonal adventures with a train of toilet tissue billowing behind it. The puppy gambols through daffodils, frolics on the beach, and bursts through piles of autumn leaves. In the most famous spot, he slides onto a frozen pond and plays with a goose. These spots are off the scale on the "aah" factor. Sure, the product looks as soft and strong as ever, but the star of the show is the puppy. He plucks irresistibly at our heartstrings.

By tapping blatantly into the emotions of the British housewife, Andrex saw off the competitive challenge until it could launch an improved product. Instead of slashing prices or employing other desperate measures, the brand's marketers sensibly decided to milk the appeal of the brand's spokesman for all the little fellow was worth. This worked so well that the brand's sales were extremely buoyant during this time of danger. What's more, every Christmas for years afterwards, a small Labrador puppy could be seen on British TV screens, sliding onto a frozen pond and playing with a goose.

Ask any focus group about Andrex and warm emotional words will come tumbling out. Quite an achievement for a toilet tissue.

The same is true of many of the world's greatest brands. Even in a research situation, it's occasionally possible to see people's eyes moisten slightly when they talk about the promise offered by Nike's vision of empowerment through sport, or Apple's celebration of independent thinking, or even Coke's hilltop depiction of global harmony. Singapore Airlines transports us into a highly evocative, long-running dream. De Beers has made its product a potent symbol of undying love. Huggies induces parents to coo at their endearingly happy babies.

Of course not all successful brands harness "big" emotions like these. But generally speaking, they conjure up a tightly defined emotional space that is very appealing and goes far beyond the brand's rational story. Even a brand that appears quite rational may be offering something deeper. The tremendous success of BMW in Britain was built on imagery that, despite to be seeming cold, tapped into powerful emotions of power, success and control. In the 1980s, Bartle Bogle Hegarty's idea of the "emotional selling proposition" recognised the importance of this emotional space.

Even science supports the importance of emotion in branding. In 2002, the Department of Psychology at the University of California, Los Angeles, published a study on how well people recognise certain words. It showed that the right side of the brain, the emotional side, played a bigger role in processing brand names than it did in processing mere nouns. This backs up what most marketers know intuitively, that emotion is fundamental to the very concept of branding.

The skilled way in which modern brands use emotion is all the more remarkable when one considers traditional corporate culture. Yes, the value of brands is understood to a greater degree than ever before, and many companies now talk about sustainability rather than short-term obsession with the bottom line. But the business world is still generally more comfortable with facts than emotions. After all, in the last decade, a concept known as "fact-based management" became quite popular. This sounds very uninspiring, but it's certainly easier for a CEO to defend than "emotion-based management." Business leaders are not expected to behave in a highly emotional fashion — not too often, anyway. Instead, they need to spend much of their time obsessing over quite rational things like product quality, product functionality and product improvement. It's only human nature that they often wish to see the results of this dedication communicated to their potential customers. It's the default position, and it's defensible in the inherently anti-emotion culture of senior management. As Mark Twain said, "It is easier to manufacture seven facts than one emotion."

However, set against this are some powerful trends which favour a more emotional approach. First, the erosion of functional product differences has been widely documented, and even where they exist, the gaps can be closed in a matter of months or even weeks. This naturally leads many brands to attempt to build a more emotional connection that is less vulnerable to an innovative competitor.

Secondly, emotions provide cut-through. In his book *The Power of Simplicity*, Jack Trout pointed out that the average manager now reads a million words a week, and refers to theories that the Baby Boomer generation is suffering significant memory loss as a result of sheer information overload. (There might be some other reasons, but that's another topic.) A few years ago, the research firm BASES reduced its predictions for the amount of awareness that could be generated by a given advertising spend. It's just not that easy to get noticed any more. In an information-saturated world, there's a lot to be said for bypassing clogged mental highways and going direct to the heart. And there's so much data around that it's easy for people to post-rationalize buying decisions that are actually grounded mainly in emotion.

Finally, the sustained success of several brands with a high emotional component to their success has simply led to a greater understanding of the power of emotion to deliver healthy financial returns. A fly on the wall of any meeting room in corporate America would hear people saying they want to "do a Nike", "a Starbucks"or "an Apple." They may not mean that they would like to imitate those companies in every respect, but they would kill for the emotional equity in those brands. Even a brand with a hideous reputation for product quality can retain such emotional equity that it can be successfully reinvented: just ask the owners of Triumph Motorcycles.

Of course many brands develop emotional equity without necessarily doing emotional advertising. Starbucks spends comparatively little on advertising, but its in-store experience is carefully planned to set off the right emotional triggers. Most brands need to rely more heavily on advertising, or at least on the broad discipline of marketing communications, to build emotional bonds. In Britain, the IPA Effectiveness Awards have encouraged particularly rigorous analysis of the effects of communications, and the real, hard-headed financial value of emotionally driven campaigns has been proven time and time again by brands as diverse as Tesco, Orange, and Andrex itself.

But hang on a minute. It can't be as easy as that, can it? (Product a little weak sir? Sales slightly droopy? That's easy sir, a little emotional bonding should do just nicely sir.) No, it's not, unfortunately. For one thing, our competitors probably have had the same idea. But more importantly, the real people we are trying to influence are not always reaching out desperately for our brand's little bundle of emotions. Enough has been written about the sophistication of modern consumers and their ability to decode and avoid every device of marketing, should they so wish. This is no longer just a phenomenon of the most advanced markets either. Siemens launched its Xelibri phone with an ironic campaign poking fun at modern technology mass-marketing and carrying the strapline "That's so tomorrow." It generated interest not just in the expected places, but also in the leading cities of China, despite their relatively recent exposure to modern marketing methods. And in the most developed markets, even irony is no longer enough. The American middle-class adoption of blue-collar brands and attitudes is simultaneously ironic and respectful: we have entered the Post-Ironic Age.

This context has made life more difficult for brands appealing through emotion. They are searching for connections with a more elusive consumer, through a communication fog of irony, self-reference and quirky humor. In a world where much advertising was quite rational, it was easier to stand out by using pure "big" emotions such as sex, excitement or the cuteness of children and animals. All these can still work, but they are received in a more sceptical environment.

Some brands have successfully reacted to this by developing campaigns, and a personality, that do not overtly use emotion in an easily described way, and yet are clearly not rational either. A successful print campaign for Diesel is based on the premise of bizarre market research conducted by the company. It uses emotion in that it makes us smile, but the humour is carefully modulated. If we think about it enough, we can figure out that it's meant to make Diesel users look like knowing, savvy people, far too intelligent to be fooled by the ludicrous methods of the marketing world. There's emotion there, but it's a far cry from the toned sexuality of Nick Kamen sitting in his underwear for Levi's in the mid-1980s.

Another development is that some brands have successfully adopted a much less predictable approach to using emotion. Their tonality is not one-dimensional, or necessarily consistent, but somehow still feels as if it's all coming from the same place. The voice of the

defining modern brand is not mono, stereophonic or even quadrophonic: it's polyphonic, like that new church organ-like ringtone on your mobile phone. It's a carefully arranged collection of emotional triggers that keeps you engaged, and adds up to a complex personality that feels real and interesting. Everywhere you look, there is evidence of the search for authenticity, massively demonstrated over the last few years by the demand for retro and vintage clothing. Polyphonic brands often feel more authentic because they feel more like real people, with a variety of moods and ways of talking.

The mother of all polyphonic brands is Nike, which has encompassed an astonishing diversity of emotions in its advertising while still talking in an inimitably Nike way. Raw excitement, tear-jerking inspiration, sophisticated and unsophisticated humour, tranquil beauty, and sheer irreverence have all played a part in Nike communications over the years. Yet, generally, you know when it's Nike talking to you and not someone else. There is a clear underlying attitude that has been imitated by many, but never consistently captured by any other brand.

This raises interesting questions for advertisers. How can they manage the process of developing a powerful polyphonic brand, which generates strong relationships by using a rich palette of emotions? The best way, of course, is if those who work with the brand have an instinctive understanding of what the brand really stands for. Nike's powerful voice has not been formed primarily by any single brand manual that dictates the emotional tone of the brand's contact with consumers. Instead, there is a hugely strong corporate culture built in part by an amazing oral tradition, which gives people who work at or for Nike a pretty good chance to get what Nike is about. Powerful emotional advertising for a brand tends to emerge when people *feel* what the brand is about, rather than do it by the manual. (Funny, that.)

It's a lot easier for this to happen when the corporate culture, the emotional heart of the company, clearly contains an essence that real people find appealing. Otherwise we may end up, as Scott Bedbury puts it, "putting lipstick on a pig." In recent years fewer advertising people have promised that advertising can solve every problem, and more stress has been put on the need to develop the right internal culture as well as the right communications. But what if the company is still a little pig-like? After all, most companies are really not that interesting to ordinary people, and many still carry a hint of a curly tail. Not every corporation can be as intuitive as Nike, Virgin or Diesel, but they still need to build strong, emotional bonds with their customers.

One response to this task is when a group of those working with the brand come together for a session to try and capture its emotional essence. In days gone by, this might have entailed going to a nice hotel in the countryside, decompressing, bonding and generally getting into a suitable state of mind. In a strict financial climate, this can often be seen as indulgent, so many "offsites" now take place onsite, in colourless conference rooms decorated by corporate art carrying inspiring symbols of teamwork or leadership. Part of the output of these sessions may be a set of guidelines for the brand's values and personality, often arranged in a circle or a box. The list of words usually looks something like this:

Honest
Confident
Contemporary
Understanding
Warm
Witty (not slapstick)
Innovative

This list goes down pretty well internally, and may be approved by consumers in research. It's difficult to argue with, and that's exactly the problem. It's incredibly bland. Consider for a moment a brand that demonstrated exactly the opposite qualities, a brand that was;

Lying
Timid
Old-fashioned
Uncomprehending
Cold
Humourless (despite occasional forays into slapstick)
Luddite

No one has launched this brand, or ever will (although I for one would buy it, if only because it sounds a lot more interesting than the first one). This reveals that many of the words most commonly used to define brand "personality" simply don't. They are just obvious. This often becomes apparent when the "personality" gets illustrated on a video "essence tape" using found footage, cut together to a rousing piece of music which no one (except Microsoft) could ever afford to use in a real piece of advertising. The results are all too often spectacularly wishy-washy. Personality and emotional richness have been eliminated, rather than enhanced.

To avoid this, those working with brands need to fight very hard to weed out the predictable or generic. We need to allow more individual, creative interpretations of a brand's personality to emerge, which are not driven by the need to achieve easy consensus. We need to use visual and aural references that feel right, rather than just illustrating a list of words. And overall, we need to allow emotions and intuition to play a bigger part in the process, since the very thing we are trying to create is itself emotional. All these are difficult in the normal course of things, but the prize, a well-defined emotional brand space, is enormously valuable.

Even if we achieve this, there may still be trouble ahead. Speed of communication, the availability of vast amounts of data on any subject, and the constantly evolving sensibilities of the people we are talking to mean that some level of rational underpinning needs to be available, even if it is not overt. If there's too big a disconnect, problems occur. At one level, the communications may simply cease to work: people may applaud the brand and like the brand for how it talks to them, but simply ignore it because their own experiences do not support the spin.

More seriously, a brand which has forged powerful emotional bonds with its audience is held up to the most stringent standards. If hell hath no fury like a woman scorned, the marketing world hath no fury like a loyal consumer scorned. The very power of Nike's emotional bonds with the American public has made it a tempting target for attack over its labour practices. Direct marketers know that some of the best customers are those who have complained and been satisfied: the disappointment of loyal customers is equally potent. However, the power of an emotionally driven relationship does not dissipate overnight and, by being seen to address those concerns over time, Nike has recaptured the lost ground.

When we say someone "is a bit emotional right now," we mean it partly as a warning. We are sending a message that "you may find dealing with this person a little difficult right now." Emotions are not always easy for people to deal with, and the same is true for brands. It's easy to make emotional advertising that is patronising, or generic, or unbelievable, or just plain nauseating. For brands, emotion brings responsibility as well as power. So it's easy to back off and fall back on advertising that appears to sell the product really well, and makes good sense in the boardroom when presented after the quarterly budget. But then you won't have a puppy on your side when the going gets tough, will you?

THE LAW OF LOVE

L ove conquers all.

Do you remember the Love Bug computer virus that swept the world a few years back? It proved that even the most hard-bitten business professionals will instantly open up an e-mail attachment simply because it came with the title "I love you," an emotional declaration that cuts straight through alertness, cognitive processes, training, security protocols and, yep, good old common sense.

"Ooh, someone out there loves me! Who, who?"

Think about this as a tick: The Love Bug didn't attack computer systems so much as human emotion, human optimism, human vulnerability, human hope.

"I love you."

Bang.

It was all over in seconds. Over 80 million computers worldwide melted down from the heart.

In lives increasingly experienced via monitors, there's a hunger for genuine empathy and direct, personal contact. People live in a cold, scary and often heartless world. Companies fire them. Spouses divorce them. Institutions stitch them up. Fear stalks the daily news. There's no one to turn to. So people want to surround themselves with sensuality.

This is the real evolution from old to new economy for marketers. Logical is being replaced by likeable. The notion of buyers and sellers is being replaced by a relationship that is better described as fan and celebrity. This transformation requires a new set of balances — not only about brand, advertising and marketing, but also about leadership, authenticity and the human spirit. Emotion is no longer a "nice-to-have" for business; rather it is the living, beating heart.

There is an incredible and untapped need for love out there. Which tells you a lot about the future of selling, argues Kevin Roberts, worldwide CEO of Saatchi & Saatchi. As Lennon sang, "Love is all you need."

The Law of Love by Kevin Roberts

"Love is the law, the law is love."
Paul Kelly

When I first said the word "Love" to serious business people, they blushed and headed for the hills. The "L" word had no place in their boardrooms and offices. Today, the response is very different. People are eager to bring more emotion, more spirit, more inspiration and, yes, more love into the way they do business. But they still find it tough to put Love in action.

That's where the idea of Lovemarks comes in — a Saatchi & Saatchi idea that puts Love into business and keeps it bubbling all around it.

I started to talk Love because of one big question that would not go away. What comes after brands? Brands have had a dream run pumping the global economy. They have defined and grown marketing by boosting its complexity and scale. They have spread out around the globe and come back home again.

The journey from products to trademarks to brands is one of the great stories of the 20th century. Now this journey is coming to an end and it's far too late for Brand-Aid. Trademarks have long been table-stakes. Now brands too are table-stakes.

Both are useful in the quest for differentiation and are still vital to survival, but they are not winning game-breakers.

It is time to admit it. Brands are dead. They are struggling to deal with the demand for innovation, flexibility and speed, together with the necessity to build close relationships with consumers. A powerful dynamic has been driving business for decades and brands are trapped in its path. It's a relentless process, turning what we truly value into the commonplace. Commodification — the process that erodes distinctions, rapidly cycles through innovations and pushes for higher standards of performance and quality because that is what everybody else is doing.

Everyone in business is wrestling with this problem in one guise or another. The inevitable result? Pressure on margins and on price at the very time consumers are pushing in the other direction. They are more demanding, less loyal, profoundly cynical and tough to convince of anything.

Most people nod at the suggestion that traditional transactions need to be transformed into relationships but they don't know what to do next. My advice is to get your nose out of reports and statistics and look to emotional connections. And, of course, look most closely at the strongest emotional connection of all — love. Love is the pathway to deep emotional connections within businesses, with consumers, with partners, with allies.

Here are eight insights that show the role Love is born to play.

Love Creates Lovemarks

Some brands are so far ahead of the pack that they have become not just "Super Brands" or "Brands Plus." They have escaped the commodity trap and evolved into something different altogether.

Charles Darwin would have got it straight off. Fish to lizard. Monkey to man. Product to Trademark. Trademark to Brand. Brand to Lovemark.

Lovemarks are a game-breaking opportunity to reinvent branding. They place brands where they should be, at the emotional heart. Lovemarks inspire loyalty beyond reason.

At Saatchi & Saatchi we have been evolving Lovemarks for the past four years. We have focused the entire company on where we want to go with them. As an Ideas Company, it is simple: "To create and perpetuate Lovemarks through the power of our ideas." Lovemarks is about attitude, belief and action. The name itself is provocative, non-negotiable. Saying "love" and believing in love come with the territory. "Enjoymarks" or "Admirationmarks" were never going to get the job done.

Lovemarks are personal. They can be local or global or anywhere in between. Whatever the scale, they stand out from the crowd. Lovemarks are the charismatic brands that people love and fiercely protect. If you made a list of Lovemarks, it would be different from mine because that is the nature of Love. We don't all love the same person either! To put my Lovemarks where my mouth is, I love Apple, Cheerios, Mont Blanc, Blackburne tennis racquets, Putumayo World Music, Tide and the Prius.

Take a few moments and share what you love on www.lovemarks.com.

Love Inspires People

All the stuff we pushed out of business in the last century needs to be enticed back to the centre. We need to feel what is important personally, not just analyze it in others. We need to transform management with Inspiration and engage both head and heart.

This is exactly what Love can do.

A study of neural activity at Emory University, Atlanta, revealed that the small act of co-operating with another person, of choosing trust over cynicism, generosity over selfishness, makes the brain light up with quiet joy. We love to love. The lead author of the study, Dr Gregory S. Berns, admitted that "The results were really surprising to us." And that is the problem. We expect the dark and suspicious side of human nature to dominate, and discount the possibility that qualities like Love and Inspiration work best.

Our traditional understanding of management has been very limited. No wonder women have found it so tough to fit in. Success today has to be about more than management and doing things right. And it has to be about more than leadership and doing right things.

What do all leaders need to succeed? Followers.

Who wants to admit to having "born to follow" tattooed on their back?

Success in business today depends not on management or on leadership but on inspiration — and at its best, Inspiration is about Love. Just as they exclude Love, most people push Inspiration out of their lives. What a terrible loss. Inspiration awakens people to their potential and shows them what they can be and what they can achieve. Inspiration is contagious and arouses people's commitment to exceed their personal best — not just to beat their sales targets or the competition.

Love is the pathway to deep emotional connections within businesses, with consumers, with partners and allies. Great products, great ideas, great anything can only come from Inspired people with passion and emotion. They need to have what I call the "I's" and the "E's."

- I for Ideas, Imagination, Intuition and Insight.
- E for Enchantment, Emotion, Empathy and Excitement.

Turning up the temperature in your business means more energy and Inspiration, and nothing turns up the temperature like Love.

Love Brings Back Emotion

We can all feel it. Emotion is back in vogue. In the grand old brand days, emotion was a clip-on. Brands flourished in the rational world of benefits. The advertising team was there to pipe on some emotional icing — and that was that. But over the past two decades, science moved deeper in the human mind. It turned out that the human brain is more complex, more densely connected and more mysterious than any of us dreamt. Study after study has proved that if the emotion centres of our brain are damaged in some way, we don't just lose the ability to laugh or cry. We lose the ability to make decisions. The neurologist Donald Calne puts it brilliantly: "The essential difference between emotion and reason is that emotion leads to action while reason leads to conclusions." More emotion equals more action. That's what the "motion" part of emotion is all about.

Now there is a big loud alarm bell for every business right there.

Emotion and reason are intertwined, but when they conflict — emotion wins every time. Without the fleeting and intense stimulus of emotion, rational thought winds down and disintegrates.

Emotion is an unlimited resource. It controls our rationality and guides our decision-making. There are no limits to its power. It's always there, waiting to be plugged into. And you certainly can't ignore it by declaring that your products are in a "low-involvement category." What a cop-out!

We need to stop talking about emotion and set it to work. We need to jump into the emotion economy. There are many openings into this economy but it is now obvious that entertainment is gaining ground fast. According to the US Consumer Expenditure survey, the total spend for entertainment per household increased 20.8% over the last decade. Entertainment appeals to our unconscious, intuitive and creative mind that operates beyond rationality and rules. Emotion and story-telling, mystery and metaphor are all central players in Lovemarks.

Love Gives Respect New Meaning

I talk more about Love than Respect because we all do Respect so much better. We have made huge investments in performance, innovation, quality, trust and all the rest for decades. And we would all agree that we made fantastic progress. The problem is that it was all in one direction towards what I call the "er" words — newer, brighter, stronger, faster. And the really big problem is that they take us head on against the most frightening "er" word of all: cheaper. This is what happens to you when you slip down the value chain. You become eager to give away more for less just to stay in the game. Even worse you put all your effort into what has just become table-stakes. Lots of puff for not much stuff.

In the 21st century, great performance is no more than what consumers expect and demand. Cars start first time, the fries are always crisp and the dishes shine. Today everyone has to earn Respect just to stay in the game.

Now the new challenge is Love, and Love demands the same investment and the same rigor we brought to the capture of Respect. Our client Toyota gets it. Don Esmond at Toyota USA crystallised the new Toyota challenge: "It's time to move from the most respected car company in America to the most loved."

Love needs Respect right from the start. Without it, we're not talking about Love, we're talking about a fad or infatuation — compelling and fun but certainly not capable of inspiring loyalty of any kind.

Love Draws on Mystery, Sensuality and Intimacy

We all know the power of mystery, sensuality and intimacy from our own lives. The obvious next question, then, is "Why should relationships in business be any different?" My answer is simple. They are not. Business too needs mystery, sensuality and intimacy. Mystery draws together the stories, metaphors and dreams that give a relationship texture. Not surprisingly, after the metric mania of the 20th century, mystery is again taking centre-stage. What we *don't* know starts to be as important as what we do know.

The five senses pull us towards sensuality — vision, sound, smell, touch, taste. This is how human beings experience the world. Sensuality is a portal to the emotions and intimacy, where thinking and feeling come together most closely; the art of knowing the right thing to do is called empathy.

Some companies have created experiences that have used mystery, sensuality and intimacy brilliantly. Think of the expertly integrated experience Starbucks has sent out around the world. Other companies have created experiences that are horribly wrong for human beings. Let's take a simple example. Who wants to be squirted with perfume as they walk into a store? Not me, and not my wife. This formulaic spray-and-bray is just a symptom of a much bigger problem — passion trimmed into efficiency. Inspiration pulled back to a positive attitude and Love diluted to "like". By focusing on mystery, sensuality and intimacy, business-as-usual can be transformed with new emotions and new ideas.

The Stanford economist Paul Romer likes to say that big competitive advantages in the marketplace always come from "better recipes, not just more cooking." Love has got to be the most well-tested recipe of all.

Love Connects with Consumers

Consumers are the heart of any enterprise, and at last, businesses are starting to realise it. People want control over their lives. They are more sophisticated and, best of all, they keep changing. This is the new consumer. To respond to this new reality requires a profound shift in how to develop ideas and insights that can truly touch consumers. What has the power to get us there? The emotional connections created by Love.

Our new evolved consumers want to connect in more ways with brands. They are looking for new emotional connections. More people are living alone and it is projected that far more will be alone over the coming decade. In the UK today, seven million adults live alone — three times as many as 40 years ago — and it is projected that, by 2020, one-person households will make up 40% of total households.

Forget Robert D. Putnam's famous "bowling alone". People are eating alone, exercising alone and waking alone. To touch these customers directly you need to listen to them. That's how you can feel the shifts in temperature, not just read about them in market research reports. Most businesses never get that close. They set up a program of consumer contact, rather than just hanging out. They take notes rather than taking the pulse.

Invest in Love and you can connect with people and you can cultivate enduring relationships. In their most evolved form, these relationships give consumers a direct impact on design, production, distribution and marketing, and give you an extraordinary new opportunity to create long-term value.

Love Revives Market Research

Researchers turned down a dead end a decade or so ago and they have been struggling to read the signs ever since. Once they had corralled what *could* be measured, everything that couldn't was simply ignored. The problem was, of course, that everything of value cannot be measured. In fact, not much of value can be. As the British industrialist John Banham once said, "We are in danger of valuing most highly those things that we can measure most accurately. As a result we are in danger of being exactly wrong rather than approximately right."

A further problem is that the information gathered by most conventional research methods has become a commodity. All the big players have access to pretty much the same information. And not only do they have the same data, they have the same processes for dealing with it. That's not where the game is going to be won and it is certainly no help in creating emotional connections with consumers.

We need research to help us discover what we don't know. And then we need research to inspire us to go further and deeper. We need research to absorb many perspectives — and make sense of them. And, most of all, we need research that puts consumers at the centre rather than at the base of a very large pyramid. This is the only kind of research that will come close enough to Love and to emotional connections to make a difference.

To have a meaningful understanding of consumers demands creativity and insight as well as accuracy and depth. Always remember that Love is not one way. You can't analyse *their* love without committing your own. If you stand to one side as an objective observer you will get the results you deserve. I'm looking for research that counts the beats of your heart rather than the fingers of your hand.

Love Loves the Local

People live in the local. They live in real, distinctive places and they love it there. I have never met a global consumer and I never expect to. We define ourselves by our differences. Differences have huge value because they are the energy of powerful emotional connections. This is the game local brands can play so brilliantly. This is also the challenge for brands with international markets.

AG. Lafley, CEO of Procter & Gamble, believes that in 10 years, P&G's toughest competitors will be focused local companies. Tell that to the global Godzillas. Mounting evidence is on their side. Take the assault on China. Four years ago, 10 of the Top 20 advertisers were global companies. Last year, just one of the Top 20 was global.

Emerging markets remain critical to growth. There are millions and millions of people wanting to take part in the ease, opportunity and spirit of the modern. But they want it their way.

International corporations do not have to retreat. Billion-dollar brands remain an inspiring goal. We certainly want more of them for our clients! We just have to get smarter.

"Think global, act local" is back-to-front.

And "Act global, think local" is not much better.

Starting with the local is absolutely right, but "think" is all wrong. "Think" is not action. "Think" is not fast or transforming, emotional or inspiring. What works better? "Act local, go global" — action at both levels.

Only Love inspires loyalty beyond reason. Lovemarks are a very simple idea. They come from deep inside what every human being wants and needs most — Love. How paradoxical that the loyalty beyond reason we are searching for should be only a heartbeat away from each of us.

THE LAW OF EXPERIENCE

Most creative people, in agencies throughout the world, have an encyclopaedic knowledge of who wrote and art directed great ads of the past, going back almost half a century. Ask about the VW ads from the 1960s, Hamlet ads from the 1970s, Apple ads from the 1980s, Nike ads from the 1990s, etc.

Ask who created the British Airways 'Face' or Tango 'Slap', Levis or Diesel, Perdue or Hathaway work. Ask them even who directed the '1984' TVC or 'Where's the beef?'

Creative people pore over award annuals, creative magazines that reproduce ads in loving detail and even, occasionally, advertising books that hero great work.

This is part of the problem.

Advertising people live in a circle of mirrors.

A great deal can be learned from the greats, no question. Case histories of all types are telling. And of course you should be a full bottle on your craft. But it's sometimes hard going forward while you're staring constantly in the rear view mirror.

It's hard to be original when you're steeped in what has been.

A walk down a creative corridor anywhere, almost anytime of day, will reveal too many noses stuck in advertising books. Stuck in the past.

It creates its own cage of conformity.

One of the first interviews I ever had with an advertising creative guru, as a young hopeful trying to break into the industry, went like this. He looked across the vast desk to me and said: "Why do you want to be a copywriter? A well educated, middle class boy like you? A comfortable Australian? Don't you know that great copywriters come the ghettos in New York? From the streets. From the Covent Garden barrow boys. People who've lived a bit and have learned a bit about life. No, Michael, you don't want to be a copywriter. Go to film school."

Like so much good advice I've received over the years, I carefully ignored it.

But he was right. You have to live before you can write.

You have to have some raw material of your own before you can create something original. The answers in the award annuals are to other peoples' questions.

Standing on the shoulders of giants is well and good. But it may give you a false perspective, an inflated sense of your own starting point.

It can also lead to advertising that is self-referential. This leaves the consumer cold. Like the annoyance you feel when others share an in-joke in front of you.

Another well-known CD gave me the benefit of his long years of experience once when he told me: "Ads get easier to write as you get older; you know which paths are going nowhere a lot quicker and which have potential."

Well, yes. If you are writing ads within the known, learnable forms of the craft maybe.

Writing ideas, however, being utterly original, is as hard the first time as the last time. The talent to be originality is a gift. But it's a bugger to unwrap.

Leading is tougher than following.

Which is why Kash Shree, now in Chicago at Leo Burnett, advocates leading an interesting life.

He'd know. It won him the Grand Prix at Cannes in 2002.

THE LAW OF EXPERIENCE BY KASH SHREE

Before I start, I'd like to ask a few questions:

Have you been arrested?

Have you exchanged stories with a stranger this week?

Have you been beaten senseless in a street fight?

Have you worked in other industries other than advertising?

Have you been fired from your job?

Have you had a near death experience?

Have you been refused service in a restaurant because of your colour?

Have you fought in a war?

Have you cried so uncontrollably that you had to vomit?

Were you picked on in school?

Did you pick on other people in school?

Have you been in a threesome?

Have you ever been lost without money in a foreign country?

Have you ever drunk a glass of vinegar?

If you can answer "yes" to at least half of these, then you may have a good understanding of my law: The law of experience.

It's a pool that you can tap into whenever you write. A very important pool. Even for advertising. Especially for advertising.

A person who's just had their heart broken sees the world differently to someone who never has and will express themselves differently. Just as a person who's been addicted to drugs sees the world differently to someone who hasn't. They just do. They're changed by their experience. Everything we experience feeds us. And because our personal experiences are usually truths of some sort. It's hard to fake that.

One of the best things I've ever done is to attend a writer's workshop with Chuck Palyhnuck (the author of *Fight Club*). Someone handed in a story of concealing traces of marijuana for an army drug test by drinking vinegar. "Did you drink vinegar when you wrote this?" Chuck asked. "Well, no" was the writer's reply. "It shows" he said.

"You can feel it when someone has actually experienced it." I believe the best work always seems to be based on some kind of truth. That's the stuff that resonates. That's the stuff that gets cynical consumers to lower their guards.

When I first joined Wieden & Kennedy I had been an avid student of advertising. I was proud of all the ads and annuals I had memorised. That was until I was confronted by Jim Riswold, a trained philosopher who had turned his hand to advertising and the writer of some of Nike's most famous ads ("Spike and Mike", "Instant Karma," "Hello World"). He wasn't a student of advertising at all. He hated advertising. He told us to throw away our annuals, study culture, then pillage it for ideas. "You don't find originality by looking at what's been done before." He was looking for unique voices not derivative ones.

Our cultures provide us with experiences which affect our personal ways of seeing things. For instance, anyone who has lived in the UK will know that the English and the French aren't terribly fond of each other. It's not something that consumes everyday thought but it's there in the national psyche, just waiting for someone to use it. And use it Howell Henry did with their ad for Black Currant Tango. It resonated so well because they had tapped into that cultural truth. I daresay this way of thinking could work somewhere else. Japan, Korea? Greece, Turkey? North and South India? It's a pretty human sentiment, after all.

A person who has grown up in Asia is going to see the world slightly differently from someone who grew up in America or England. That doesn't mean we're all so different and will never understand one another. I don't subscribe to the view that only Asians know how to advertise to an Asian market. It's as short-sighted as thinking that only Europeans know how to advertise to a European market. People are more similar than they are different. There's far more unifying us than separating us. We all want to love. Be loved. We all eat. We all want security. And we all like to buy stuff. The contexts may change but people generally don't.

Our cultures help shape our ways of seeing things. And different ways of seeing things are a valuable resource in advertising where we all feel like we've seen everything before. About 10 years ago, Sweden started to appear on the world advertising map. They had a strange way of looking at things, to say the least. And it showed in their work. The Diesel advertising coming out of Paradiset in Stockholm was hugely successful. The Swedish agency's strangely kitsch and ironic point of view turned out to be really appealing to a cynical Generation X. Traktor, a group of Swedish directors responsible for producing much of the Diesel work became the most sought-after directors in the world. In turn, their work started to influence advertising in the US and the UK.

But what happens when you displace some of those Swedes and put them in a new environment? Would they still be different? Would they be understood? Two of the Diesel creatives, Linus and Paul ventured to the US to try their hand at Fallon. Here's a little of what they did.

It didn't look like anything else in the US, which meant it stood out like the proverbial dogs' balls. And, once again, helped change advertising a little more over there.

Other creatives and agencies started trying to do more kitsch and ironic work. Remember the C-Net campaign from Leagus in San Francisco and the Discovery.com campaign from Hal Riney? Both campaigns incidentally, directed by Traktor. They had changed the industry in the US by showing them a new voice.

When Neil French first turned up in Singapore, he brought a unique voice that changed the market there. When you mixed that up with Australians like Jim Aitchison, the style started to evolve further. The next generation helped bring Singapore its own flavour. People Like Calvin Soh and Francis Wee took those European and Australian influences and brought their own sensibilities and experiences to them. Thanks to all that influencing and cross-fertilisation, Singapore now has it's own definitive advertising style.

Advertising is always better when you try to mix things up. Wieden & Kennedy did it in throughout the 90s. They brought in non-advertising people and made them work with ad people. They brought in designers and architects and mixed them up with philosophers and just plain odd people. Say what you like about their work then, but you can't accuse it of being like anyone else's. It was unique. It was honest. It was thoughtful and funny and ironic and provocative. It wasn't like advertising.

They also brought athletes to work on the advertising. They realised that sport was a culture with its own truths. And if you weren't being· authentic, then your audience would reject you.

No one wants to hang out with a phoney.

Of course, the Swedes weren't the first group of invading foreigners to help diversify advertising voices. There were Australians going to the UK and the US a decade or so earlier. Eugene Cheong and Tan Shen Guan had ventured over to the UK to try and add their voices to the mix. And we've already talked about Neil.

So what happens when you start taking voices out of Asia and get them to apply some of their thoughts and memories in the Western market? Well, a good example is Tarsem's "Elephant" spot for Coke. He had seen elephants swimming while growing up in India and it added a fresh image to most of our visual psyches. Because you don't see many swimming elephants in Atlanta.

I'm going to bastardise a Tarsem quote, but I think it's an important insight into what we do. "You don't pay me for the film I shoot or the awards I've won. You pay me for every book I've read. My childhood. Every walk I've taken, every movie I've seen." With changing emigration and more open, diverse, worldly media, more foreign and alien experiences start to overflow and permeate into other cultures. You start to see some interesting imagery come from unexpected places. The Peugeot Sculptor spot was from an Italian agency, for a French car, with an Indian theme.

I went to Singapore in 1992 because, while at O&M London, I had heard about Eugene Cheong and Shen Guan. Well, to be honest I had heard that they said it was really easy to sell work out there. Of course they were lying. But still it got me to up and leave. That and being fired from my job in London.

So I brought my own set of experiences and ways of seeing to Singapore, and had my ways of seeing changed by the place. The more places I live in, the more different ways of seeing things I'm exposed to. Even if I misinterpret them, I'm still changed. And, just perhaps, more unique. And the more unique I become, the more valuable I become.

For example, in England when the sun comes out, we all rush to try and soak in as many rays as possible. Because we never know when we're going to see it again. So imagine my surprise when I go out walking with my wife, who is from India. And she starts taking this really convoluted route to get to places. The sun's not such a big treat for her. In fact, she tries to avoid it at all costs. I'd be saying, "Where are you going, the shops are over here?" Andy, my old partner, experienced the same thing when he moved to Singapore. He was astounded too.

Well, you store that stuff away. Until one day you write a spot about a woman running a convoluted route to stay in the shade. I doubt whether Andy or I would have known that without having observed things in Asia. Little things.

So what happens when you get an Indian kid from Singapore, send him over to England at the age of seven months, "bring him up with West Indians, and then get him to live and work in four different continents? Hopefully you get a different way of seeing things.

So what am I getting at? Don't be closed. Look for new experiences. Reals ones, preferably. If you can, don't go straight from school, to college to advertising. Get arrested first. Leave the country. Go out and take your experiences elsewhere. Then come back changed and apply that new modified voice at home. Or somewhere else again.

I used to train as a martial artist. And would do everything with my feet. The experience ended up being a soccer ad for Nike.

(What are you getting ready for?)

Drunk and bored at a Christmas party once, I decided to piss off my friend's dog who had been following me around. I decided to follow it around until it snapped. It took about 45 minutes. And I did get bitten. But 17 years later it became the inspiration for Tailgating.

THE LAW OF RELEVANCE

I know some clients accuse creativity of occasionally committing the crime of irrelevance. However, the reality is that your advertising message is competing with, well, reality. Your ad must not only be more interesting than other ads. It must be more immediately compelling than the editorial or programming surrounding it.

Way beyond that, your ad must also be more interesting than the other things in life that demand our attention.

Relevance, like beauty, is in the eye of the beholder. Frequently, what advertisers think is as relevant, as compared to what customers think, is as different as chalk and cheese. To a client, his ingredients are important. The glossy features. The beauty shot. Fact is, everyday humans have a much broader palette of emotions than advertisers. To a consumer, only the solution to their emotional problem is important.

The Law of Relevance is not about glib product correctness; it doesn't matter how right, earnest or worthy the advertising is if it's too dull to be noticed.

Great ads have impact, but they also pay attention to the feelings that are being generated by the idea.

Impact is a start — the only possible start, really. Invisibility is death, but so is a lack of clarity, or creating impact without creating likeability, or a lack of emotional relevance.

If your ads don't reach out to people, then people won't reach for your products.

It's not enough just to make and sell products anymore. Nike's Phil Knight said, "There's no value in making things anymore. The value is added by innovation and marketing."

Great ads are difficult to define, but they all probably have an element of novelty (they do the unexpected), they generate positive feelings (they are likable), and they have meaning (they are relevant).

Remember REG (Respect, Empathy, Genuineness)? If your ad has achieved these three things, then you're using the force of the Law of Relevance. Laws like Simplicity, Humour and Irreverence, are ways to reveal a truth in your idea; whereas, Laws like Positioning, Respect and Relevance ensure this insight is warmly and enthusiastically received.

Things that are relevant to the product can be irrelevant to the market. People want to know about their beautiful flowers, not about the phosphate levels in your manure.

The TV networks knows this. In late 2003, the US NBC found a new way to get people to stay with the paying commercial in the ad breaks — by interspersing minute-long "movies" among the ads and prime-time shows, supplying the stories, mystery, emotion and all the instinctive nourishment that the ads weren't.

In what follows, Anne Bologna, Harvard tutor and president of the US Fallon network, cites Citibank's work as an example of relevance that started out to be "refreshingly unbanklike." How was this relevant? Because the campaign focussed on what was relevant to people; where other banks show money, Citibank showed real life.

Real life; that always passes the relevancy test.

THE LAW OF RELEVANCE BY ANNE BOLOGNA

People don't read ads,
they read what interests them and sometimes it's an ad.
George Gossage

Great advertising happens when creativity and relevance meet. A good ad can be creative but not relevant, or relevant but not creative, but precious few are both. Unfortunately, most are neither. You know an ad is relevant when it makes someone stop and pay attention to what is, essentially, an uninvited intrusion. In the past, ads weren't necessarily uninvited intrusions. In many cases, today, ads are actually welcome diversions, providing educational insights for people who are seeking information about a specific product or service. But how do you make people find relevance in an advertising message?

First, let's put "advertising" and "relevance" into context. In the 1950s everything was relevant. In the years after World War II, it seemed there was nothing that wasn't relevant to the lives — and lifestyles — of returning GIs and their new families: toothpaste, cookies, canned foods, automobiles, lawn mowers, washing machines. Was there anything that wasn't relevant to these new families and their Baby Boomer children? Everyone not only wanted everything, but they needed it all, and even better was the fact that everything being created was for the most part brand new. And the new technologies: television, air conditioning, the Colgate Gardol Shield, provided relevance in every way, shape or form.

Who could deny that when Crest Toothpaste showed a smiling Norman Rockwell-esquire, all-American child, bringing home his dental report card and exclaiming, "Look Mom, no cavities" that this wasn't the height of relevance? After all, millions of American parents with millions of Baby Boomer children certainly didn't want to spend extra money on dentists. So when Crest claimed it prevented more cavities than any other brand of toothpaste, Moms took notice.

Everything in the 50s seemed to have a real product difference, and everything was relevant to our lives in those days. Was it creative? Well, not in the terms of how we see creativity today. But it was quite emotional, hitting on a topic dear to parents' hearts.

As America began to build a supercharged economy in the 1960s, along came for many people disposable income. Though poverty was still rampant in the country, the years of war deprivation were soon replaced by a new economy, one where people could purchase new products that did new things, where they had some money left over after each week's paycheck went for necessities. But there was more to life in America in the 1960s. Civil rights became a major issue for the nation, and as a war in Southeast Asia escalated, the 1960s and everything in America and the world began to change, including the way we communicated.

As creativity became the buzzword in films, television, music and art (think of the enormous energy and remarkable innovations in 1960s pop and high culture), it was only fitting that advertising would also produce messages that not only sold products and established brand names, but became cultural icons on their own. "You don't have to be Jewish to love Levy's" may have been an early example of cultural diversity — or political incorrectness. Yet it sold lots of bread, and at the same time, established a brand and created a buzz.

Alka Seltzer and Volkswagen consistently pushed the limits of creativity, offering the public mini "feature films" complete with story lines and dénouements, all within a 60-second time frame. For anyone who had ever suffered heartburn, there was nothing more relevant. "Whatever Shape Your Stomach's in" produced a hit song, "Speecy Spicy Meatball", made fun of the advertising business, "Marshmallowed Meatballs" parodied the bride who couldn't cook. Each was entirely relevant.

When Doyle Dane Bernbach created the advertising for Volkswagen, they not only made extraordinary short films, "The Funeral," they also created a style of print advertising that was clean, simple, elegant, and actually communicated fun via typeface and style. That format remains the standard. It was not only topical back in the 1960s, but it endures today, in a manner that is both timeless and yet remains fresh some 40 years later. When the new VW Bug was launched just a few years ago, the print ads were done in the original VW print format, slightly updated, but still looking as fresh, and as new as when this campaign was born.

The Early to Mid-60s Brought Us the First Law of Relevance: Creativity

As the Vietnam War rose in our consciousness and arrived in our homes each night via television, the Baby Boomer generation set out to change the world. Demanding peace, social justice, sex, drugs, rock and roll, long hair, a sense of fun and at the same time, a sense of outrage, the Boomers made for great visuals, lots of ink in the press and even more importantly, a new way of marketing.

While demographics had been a part of the advertising business for years, the generation gap provided new markets, new attitudes and psychographics. No longer were age and income the prime filters for targeting and reaching a specific audience. Now there were attitudes involved — lifestyles. Marketing products to people based on their interests rather than how much money they earned brought marketers into a new age, and opened the door for creating products based on desire, rather than simply need. In remembering those times, it's clear that relevance then became a generational issue. For what was relevant to the "youth of America" wasn't necessarily relevant to their parents or their government. But it was relevant to the record companies, apparel makers, cigarette rolling paper companies and so many others who studied the market and learned how best to approach them.

The Law: I Know Your Market ... Well

By the 1970s relevance was not only generational and political, it was gender-based, sexuality-based, multicultural and personal...very personal. What was political became personal, and as Boomers decided they couldn't change the system, they would change themselves instead. Thus was born the "Me Decade," so named because out of the chaos of the 1960s was born a period of intense inner and outer scrutiny. We embraced the causes that had personal meaning to us and then we took every possible workshop, seminar and course to make ourselves "better." And it didn't matter if one was offering education, inspiration, motivation or products and services. If it wasn't relevant to the audience in question, it simply wasn't relevant — unless the media said it was! And the media told us that fixing our minds and our bodies was the greatest way to ultimately fix society.

Of course, the Boomers still wanted products that reflected their inherent "differences" from their parents. So smart marketers offered products to the "Me Generation" that were functionally similar but designed to appear different... or designed to reflect the growing concerns over what would soon become known as "political correctness."

World events, too, began to shape what was truly relevant, portending the 21st century. When the gas crisis hit the US in the late 1970s those most prepared were the car makers who were selling cars that ran 30-40 and, yes, even 50 miles per gallon. The US was no longer living in a vacuum as cause and effect caught up with them. What occurred overseas and in places they didn't quite understand had a direct effect on their daily lives. And what was really relevant in the world was what was relevant in their product selections.

The Law: Understand the World, Understand Trends.
They *Do* Affect the Marketplace

As the "Me Decade" gave way to the 1980s, the Boomers were forced to start growing up and acting their age. There was already a backlash against the Baby Boomer generation's lust for staring at their navels, and then complaining to the media about it. But what the media failed to notice, *Rolling Stone*, and their ad agency in Minneapolis certainly picked up on. Perception/reality clearly depicted the media stereotypes of the *Rolling Stone* readership — and then did one better by showing the reality. It was the most perceptive communication about this audience, and truly helped set the stage for the changes about to come.

And what changes. The Boomers' contemplation of their own heads beget the "Yuppies" who didn't seem to care about anything but money, status, money, status and of course, power. "Greed is good," proclaimed Gordon Gecko in the movie *Wall Street* and everyone it seemed, putting aside any sense of discipline when it came to spending money, until of course, October 1987, when the market bottomed out, giving them time to anticipate the next boom. Who would have dreamed that it would be fuelled by technology and powered by a group of millionaires who rewrote the rules because they were too young to have learned them?

What grew out of the dotcom mania? We're still looking for answers. But it's clear that younger people — the "Generation Ys" — having been so inundated by media and marketing their entire lives, were a bit jaded and cynical about products and the corporations behind those products. They saw virtually everything become commoditised and so what became more important was the way corporations behaved. "Was this a corporation I could work for? Do they share my values? Do they have a worldview I admire?" That became the mantra that led to marketers studying emotional branding and how best to make consumers emotional about their brands!

The Law: Commodities Can Have a Special Place in Peoples Lives

With this in mind, corporations need to communicate their corporate values and their place in the world to their audiences. Emotional connections are important to today's consumer even when the products are commodities.

The good news for advertising folks is that, as we've seen in this brief and skewed history, human beings are a pretty self-centred lot, so it's not that difficult to make your message relevant. The truth is people spend most of their daily lives seeking to satisfy a host of personal needs. Every example already cited demonstrates this point, even with the filters of various trends and times. Some needs are relatively trivial, though we think they're rather important: like the need to get a date, a raise or to be in the know. On a more fundamental level, people need to be loved, to belong and to feel safe. Once we have an understanding of needs and desires, we can reach out to our audiences with more clarity and more relevance.

As times changed, as we've become more sophisticated about how to create and tailor messages to reach our markets, one thing remains the same: The ability to communicate a product or service message in a way that's relevant is the essence of advertising. It's also the essence of all good communication. And in the case of advertising, it is, of course, good communication and the art of persuasion.

Here is an example of good communication, great persuasion and true relevance: Citibank — "an advocate for a healthy approach to money." How did Citibank and its agency arrive at this provocative strategy? By using all the laws of relevance cited.

Top Line: Finally, there's a bank that actually understands there's more to life than money.

Citibank: A Brand Miles Wide and Inches Deep.

A successful business on virtually any measure, Citibank competes in the most undifferentiated categories: credit cards and banking.

Worse yet, consumers typically think of banks like utilities — convenience drives choice. And while consumers love the spending power of credit cards, they hate the motivations of companies behind them. So there's little reason to care about "issuing bank" brands. After acceptance, card choice comes down to rates and fees.

A brilliant way to convince people you're different is to act different. From the outset, the charge has been dauntingly clear: help Citibank stand apart. Communications must give consumers a reason to care about and prefer a brand that wouldn't normally get a second thought.

Objectives:
(1) Distinguish Citibank from card, banking and financial services brands.
(2) Demonstrate relevance to consumer's lives.
(3) Predispose people to use or acquire Citibank offerings.

But first, they had to find someone who would listen.

In a culture that elevates money to godliness, Citibank's best prospects don't buy it. Looking at society, you'd think money drove America. Initial discussions of money led straight to expected places like "freedom" and "control." So we asked consumers about life instead: what makes a good life? What's the secret to everyday happiness? How much money is enough? Suddenly, a different view of money emerged. We found people with realistic goals, making sacrifices to stay balanced. For them, personal prosperity didn't equal money. Money was a means to an end. Financial success was living happily within your means. We called this group "Balance Seekers." Best of all, research showed they represent almost half of adults and were great financial prospects.

There's more to life than money.

Unsurprisingly, Balance Seekers were frustrated by the bank's blatant self-interest. "Are they going to ask about my money or my life? Because if all they're interested in is my money then I'm not interested." They were interested in a bank that helps them live rich lives — not get rich. A bank that understood life comes before money. We described their outlook as a "healthy approach to money."

The tooth fairy? Leprechauns? A credit card that helps you balance your finances? Credit cards remained challenging. Credit is inherently "unhealthy"; it implies spending beyond your means. Because companies promote plastic as worry-free money, Balance Seekers felt victimised. "They just want you to spend, spend, spend. That's how they make money." In research, Balance Seekers likened cards to a "genie in a bottle," powerful but tricky. They didn't trust themselves to resist the genie's temptation to spend. Instead, they just kept the lid on the bottle.

"I only carry one card in my wallet at a time." The others still exist but rarely see the light of day.

That seemed unhealthy too, not to mention bad for Citibank's business. We asked if there was middle ground between denial and over-spending, a "healthy" way to use cards. Balance Seekers told us the key was using cards wisely.

"Being able to earn rewards for using your cards is wise."

"Using your card to get purchase protection or travel insurance is a good use."

"I need to be informed about how cards work."

"If a card could help me keep tabs on my spending, that would be healthy."

Grounding card communications in these ideas not only connected credit to a "healthy approach," but also provided a link to tangible features.

A Simple Fact: No One has Ever Been Bored into Buying Anything.

Citibank asked for "refreshingly unbank-like" advertising. That opened the door to offer a contrast to the credit card category. As a result, where most bank ads were serious, Citibank found humour. While banks talked about themselves, they focused on people. And when banks showed money, they showed real life.

Being "unbank-like" also means avoiding media that objectify money. In diaries, Balance Seekers described their media habits and passions: home, family, health, community, and personal growth. Citibank's message connects perfectly with media that reflect these priorities: lifestyle magazines versus business and finance publications.

Just When Everything Seems Under Control, Life Happens. And When Life Happens What Have We as Marketers Learned from the Citibank Campaign?

Citibank's campaign was launched in 2001, the era of irrational exuberance, just as the dotcom bubble was about to burst. And right before the bubble burst, it seemed that for many people, there was only one thing in life: money. Yes, there were businesses where there were onsite massages, football tournaments, drinking till dawn, three hours of sleep a night, but that was because the stress to produce, the pressure from the investors, the almost maniacal hysteria surrounding the bottom line (or lack thereof) demanded release and relief. Citibank agreed to run a campaign saying there was ... there is ... more to life than money, a message that seemed counter to the prevailing mood.

But that was 2001. By 2002, we all knew that there was and always will be more to life than money. And now, two years later, the human truths of the Citibank campaign are all the more relevant to us, banking consumers and marketers alike. For what is relevance but revealing these human truths in a manner that talks to us, reaches us, persuades us and touches us? It's what good advertising really is all about.

THE LAW OF HUMOUR

One of America's most successful exports has been canned laughter. It's the staple diet of the world's sitcoms, home video shows, comedies, and is now even used in children's shows. I'm amazed it's not used in TV commercials (other than ironically).

After all, telling the audience at home when something is funny would be useful in many TVC scripts, who seem to think they're being funny when they seriously aren't.

There's a thing I call ad-funny. It's when something is only funny to the ad people who made it. It's not "real funny," because it's really not funny. Perhaps real people have a higher funny bone threshold than ad people; how else can so many unfunny scripts be classified as comedy?

Why are there so many clichéd caricatures masquerading as wit? Goofy voices and stupid expressions aren't funny; they're forced and fake. Most radio commercials fall into this category.

And many formula-driven TV spots too. It has given humour a bad name with some advertisers.

A client once accused me of using humour as a first resort. I lamely explained that creative teams don't always set out to write a humorous idea, but rather, when you're searching for the shortest, sharpest way to express a thought, the answer is often a compression of a couple of different notions. This synthesis is often surprising and elicits the humour of surprise.

Clive James, who once famously described the Californian Governor, Arnold Schwarzenegger, as looking like a bunch of walnuts wrapped in a condom, said he wasn't trying to be funny at the time. He was simply trying to "describe properly," to convey something in the least number of words.

Compression leads naturally to humour. And, happily, humour leads naturally to a smile. An example of how important smiles are comes from a Chinese hospital that recently reported a significant drop in the number of complaints, after ordering staff to show at least eight teeth while smiling at patients.

Humour is so powerful in advertising (when it *really* is funny) because it's a bridge that links the brand and the consumer. Laughter, it's been said, is the shortest distance between two people.

A smile is a meeting of minds.

Now, that's truly interactive advertising.

A smile means your audience is literally and physically responding to the message (and by association, the advertiser behind it), and engaging with it in a positive way.

Wit invites participation. Humour makes an ad more likely to be repeated by word of mouth. Even better, it makes people feel more comfortable talking about and recommending the brand because, in a very real way, they've taken part in a little of the brand experience.

Humour also adds fame and topicality to the brand when people say, "Did you see that ad where ..."

Humour is the point where your brand's personality is at its most human, touching a facet of your audience's personality and tickling their fancy as well. More than any other sales tool, humour invokes a special kind of collective intimacy. In brief, it's a shortcut to being a likeable brand.

The problem is that advertising is not always very good at it. Many clients would like to produce funny ads, but business today is serious. Jokes are hard to justify in rationale-driven meetings. If you're going to go funny with your campaign, you better make sure it's a real giggle on the cold, pale page, even when the account executive reads it out aloud.

Different countries, like people, find different things funny, which is why national or even parochial campaigns are usually better at humour than global campaigns. An interesting aside, here, is the example of Australian beer advertising. Australians are widely known to like a laugh and love a beer or two. Yet, for decades, much Aussie beer advertising was turgid, try-hard, and stubbornly unfunny. It took an Englishman to show the way.

M&C Saatchi founding partner, James Lowther's UK campaigns for Australian brands like Foster's and XXXX used the classic drollery of the Aussie personality to hugely successful, and humorous, effect.

Here, he discusses the Law of Humour, after talks with the creator of some of the funniest things in the world: God.

THE LAW OF HUMOUR BY JAMES LOWTHER

Claud Hopkins once said, "People don't buy from clowns."

At that point the clouds opened, a deep vibrant voice spake "Wrong, Claud love," and deposited several thousand tons of Volkswagens, crates of John Smiths, Foster's, Stella Artois, Budweiser, Tango, a BA jumbo jet and a whole lot of drunk patrons of Club 18-30 to mention but a few upon his distinguished pate. If he had survived the incident, Claud would undoubtedly have revised his opinion.

Humour, not only wins most of the awards at most festivals, but also wins more business for clients than any other tool in the advertiser's armoury.

Why?

Because logic can make you think a product is a sensible choice. But only humour can make you like it.

Because only humour requires the actual *participation* of the viewer, so he/she is more likely to remember it.

And because fish swim, snakes bite, pandas eat bamboo, they all have sex ... but only humans laugh.

Laughter is the common currency that humans use to make life seem better. Advertising is trying to persuade people that their products make life better. So the alliance of the two is a match made in heaven.

Speaking of heaven, that same voice spake unto me on the mountaintop – well, Golden Square actually — and did burn a few commandments about humour upon my Quark Express in letters of fire. After IT had put out the conflagration, I set them down for this esteemed publication.

1 Thou Shalt Love Thy Neighbour — He's Dead Funny

The best jokes and the best ads aren't based on imagination. They're based on observation, observations of those funny creatures all around us ... people. (If we want to get our products into people's lives, we'd better know about them). So the first thing to do before you pick up a piece of paper, is look at the world and the people around you. No, not the Groucho club... real people. See how they speak, how they gesture, how they tell

whoppers, how they kiss and fart and how they never look at each other in a lift. (That's why they've never found Lord Lucan. He's hiding in a lift.) And how they use, talk about or behave with your product. And I'm not talking about research. I'm talking about you, the creative person, observing.

The campaign I'm proudest of is Castlemaine XXXX. It's based on a time when I was 17, working for seven months as a Pommy jackeroo on an Australian sheep station way out in the outback.

Other than losing my virginity and learning how to dag a sheep and cheat at poker, I also learned that outback Australians never use a polite word when an obscene word will do … and that in temperatures of 40 degrees, a cold beer is more important than your mates, women and often life itself.

Some 15 years later, we came up with the line "Australians wouldn't give a XXXX for anything else." The scripts that came out of this needed a bit of imagination. But the characters didn't. They were already there.

Handy hint: When you see anyone do something strange or funny, write it down. You can nick it and use it later.

2 Thou Shalt not Kill … but Wounding is Quite a Laugh

Neil Simon once said, "All humour is based on hostility. That's why World War II is so funny."

Other than the questionable conclusion, the observation is faultless. If we're honest, there's nothing that constitutes a greater source of pleasure than the weaknesses or misfortunes of others. In advertising, it can be used to great effect to get people to remember your brand name. (Who can forget the logo of Outpost.com after seeing live gerbils being fired through it?)

It can be used to dramatise a product benefit. (Recently, in a Foster's tactical ad, we used a crocodile decapitating a bungee jumper to demonstrate how our new hit pump stops the beer losing its head.)

It can also be used to assail the weaknesses of your real or imagined rivals. (Witness the magnificently painful foreign games lampooned by Fox TV.)

And some time ago, I used it for Schweppes to parody other people's advertising, with John Cleese as the assassin. At the time Calvin Klein was leading a vogue for pretentious black and white ads with equally pretentious and meaningless dialogue. Schweppes had a culture of dry and ironic ads, but we wanted it to be more modern. What better way to put yourself alongside but, at the same time, above modern icons but unmercifully and woundingly extracting the piss from it. So we took the slightly meaningless…and turned it into total but very beautifully photographed bollocks.

Handy hint: When doing parody, you have to execute it as well as the original. And do it seriously. Just take it to absurd extremes.

3 Thou Shalt not Bear False Witness

Did you read right? Is this guy telling you to tell the TRUTH! Yes, you did. And yes I am.

At the beginning of these tablets, the man up there said that the reason humour and advertising make such good stalemates is that the best examples of both are based on observation. In other words, they're based on truth.

Many people outside our business and I suspect some inside, think advertising is about "creative lying." But the best ads are actually based on truth. They have to be, otherwise people will not believe them and will not buy the products. And that's why good humour and good advertising so often go hand in hand.

Here I must distinguish between "factual" and "truthful."

The great American humorist PJ O'Rourke said "Humour is by its nature more truthful than factual." Humorous ads may exaggerate the facts, abuse or ignore them to get at the truth, but at the core of the idea is a truth to which people can say, "Yes, it is like that."

And funnily enough, the best example our agency has of this is an ad we did for BA with PJ himself. Here he paints a picture of Britain as a dog-obsessed, rain-soaked country, where we eat revolting curry and invent games that no one understands and then get beaten by the rest of the world at them, in other words, the truth … albeit somewhat selective & embellished.

When he sets this against the fact that we also have the world's favourite airline, you will believe that too.

The only thing I resent is his assertion that we prefer tea to sex. But then, I drink coffee and have four kids.

Handy Hint: After writing your script, ask yourself if it's funny up front. Then ask yourself if it's true underneath. Well, a bit true.

4 Thou Shalt Commit Adulteration

According to the dictionary, adulteration is making something impure by adding foreign or incongruous substances to it.

And that is exactly what comedy does.

PG Wodehouse said, "Comedy is the kindly contemplation of the incongruous." And Max Sennet put it even more revealingly, "humour is when an idea going in one direction meets an idea going in the opposite direction." So if you want to do a funny and

revealing ad, try putting two wildly different things together. And the key here is what I call the "what if" question.

With our Foster's campaign, we asked, "what if" people of different nationalities drank Foster's and started behaving like Australians?

So, we wrote the line: "He who drinks Australian, thinks Australian," and then we had a Frenchman treating a beautiful woman like a baggage handler, a German asking his kidnapped wife where she put the golf clubs and a Japanese robot in a threesome with a can of beer, a vacuum cleaner and a microwave oven.

In Australia, our guys asked "what if" you tried to find another way of saving as much money as you do with ANZ bank? We had a woman, blacking in the hole in her tights with magic marker.

In my late night imaginings, I wonder "what if" Romeo and Juliet were only able to conduct their love affair with text messages? So I want to do a series of "The Classics on text." ("What if" you tried to nick this idea? I'd sue.)

Handy hint: Take your product and look at it not from the point of view of the client or even the agency. But from the point of view of the consumer ... or a vet or trapeze artist or underwater brain surgeon ... or ... well you get the idea.

5 Thou Shalt Use Lots of Graven Images ... Visual Gags Rule, OK

Back in the caves, before satire, parody, irony and pathos or any other words for that matter, had been invented, nothing would make your average Neanderthal giggle quite as much as a mate's animal skin falling down while he was chasing a hairy mammoth or the like. To complete his joy, the mate would then trip over his animal skin (they didn't have banana skins in those days) and do himself severe damage.

The sight gag or visual humour is born.

Thousands of years later, having invented language, philosophy, the internal combustion engine, flight, television, quantum physics and those machines that serve tennis balls at you, humans still just adore sight gags.

Here are a couple of stories to illustrate how you can never underestimate the hilarity of a good old-fashioned Pratt fall.

I have done a talk called "Laughing All the Way to the Bank: How Humour Sells" in three wildly different places. California, Shanghai and South Africa. In them I would talk about different styles of humour, showing films that illustrate each style and then measuring the response from the audience with a "laughometer"... actually just a sound meter but hey, we all know how important the brand name is.

In the visual humour section, I would show the famous Hamlet phone booth ad, the Fox Sport "If only Golf was Hockey" ad and a Dutch ad for the football pools, which shows a man pretending to open a glass door for someone and laughing his rocks off when the guy nearly knocks himself out walking into the door. In Monterey, Shanghai and Johannesburg, these got the biggest laugh of the lot.

And here's an example from my own experience. In our Calvin Klein spoof for Schweppes, much of the humour comes from the deadpan nonsensical dialogue, executed as only John Cleese can.

Cleese: "Why do we walk like one dancer in a dream?"

Woman: "Because, when I step on your shadow, it is I that feels the pain." And so on ad nauseam.

The script called for the girl to slap John once, a la Calvin Klein. Paul Weiland than asked her to punch him in the solar plexus as an extra visual gag.

When we cut the film together, there was a lot of debate about whether the solar plexus punch was too obvious, crude and generally OTT. So we tested two versions of the film, one with the punch, one without.

Not only did the "with punch" version win, but the punch was the precise moment in the film when silent amusement exploded into audible laughter.

The ad went on to win the ad of the year at the British Television awards.

Handy hint: Most of the time, aspire to do something witty, challenging and intelligent. But every so often, a crass, primitive punch in the goolies is well in order.

6 People Coveting Their Neighbour's Ass Is Always Good For A Giggle

Someone once wrote, "genitals are a great distraction to scholarship." (That may explain my rather feeble grades at university.) But no one would describe sex as a great distraction to selling. As everyone knows, sex is, in an unfortunate expression once used to me, "a powerful tool for the adman."

But here, I'm not talking about the sex that stirs up the hormones, but sex that tickles that other bone — the funny bone, for, the fact is that sex is as likely to raise a snigger as anything else.

In the 18th century, Lord Chesterton said of sex: "The pleasure is momentary, the position ridiculous, the expense damnable." The old codger had a point, and even today, you can sell people onto something by playing on that shared recognition that sex can not only be magnificent fun, but magnificently funny.

Who can forget, the magnificent Braathens Airline ad advertising their half-price fares for in-laws, where the randy husband kicks off his pants, grips a rose in his teeth and bursts into the room to offer his wife a good seeing to only to confront the father and mother-in-law in mid-sip of their Earl Grey?

I myself broached the subject of potential homosexual fellatio in my Mafia Foster's ad, "Kiss."

And guys laughed. Except the ones with moustaches.

Handy hint: Observe the absurdity and humour of sex. But, unless you're prepared to risk embarrassing physical damage, don't tell your partner you're doing it.

7 Thou Shalt Keep Thy Gag Unto Thyself Until The End

Charlie Chaplin's definition of the best gag is:

> Banana skin on pavement
> Man walking towards banana skin
> Man about to step on banana skin
> Man sees banana skin at last moment
> Man steps around the banana skin with a self-satisfied smile
> And falls down manhole.

You think you're watching one thing. You think it's over. Kerbang! Something else happens. Surprise. And the same goes for ads. Build up a situation piece by piece towards the anticipated ending. Then, at the last minute, turn the whole contraption on its head and whip the carpet from under it.

This is particularly useful, when you are trying to dramatise a product benefit by comparing it to something precisely the opposite.

Our Australian agency provided one of the best examples of yanking the Axminster, with their client Berri orange juice, who tells us: "The goodness is in the glass."

In one, lovely granny is trying to tie her shoelaces. Adorable grandson, with an expression to melt the heart of Martin Boorman, kneels down to do it for her. He gives her a big hug and we close on the face of grandma, touched almost to tears. We pan down to her feet to see the little bastard has tied her shoelaces together.

In another one, a proud dad watches his little angel mowing the lawn. After a suitably vitamin enriching swig of his Berri orange juice, the kid struggles on manfully, until he has completed his task of mowing the word "Shit" into the sward.

The little s**t could have mowed Berri's sales increase chart into the lawn... but that would have needed a bigger lawn.

Handy hint 1: The best way to conceal your intentions is to make the front very charming or emotional and execute it as seriously as if that were the whole story. The bigger the contrast with the end, the bigger the drop, the funnier the ad.

Handy hint 2: Surprise can hurt. When once talking on humour in Monterey, I decided to give a personal demonstration of the Charlie Chaplin theory. Before I mounted the stage, I placed a banana skin in plain view by the podium. In the absence of a manhole cover, I decided that I would fall over my chair to make the point. I duly ascended the stage, walked past the banana skin with a self-satisfied smirk, fell over the chair and pulled three tendons in my knee.

8 Thou Shalt Honour Thy Product

One of our clients once used to draw himself up to his full height when briefing us, and warn us in apocalyptic tones, that he didn't want his scripts to be "one of those sponsored jokes." At the time, I found this all rather depressing. But now I know precisely what he had meant.

To tell a joke in 30 seconds and then sticky tape a product on the end is a crappy ad.

If it's a brilliant joke, but it is just an appendage to make the ad more watchable, it's still a crappy ad.

The best ads and funniest ads happen when the joke comes from the product and actually could not exist without the product.

The XXXX ads would not be funny, unless they were demonstrating our line that "Australians wouldn't give a XXXX for anything else."

The antics of Danny Kleinman's great bear-fighting salmon fisherman are made not only relevant but funnier by the fact that they are demonstrating the lengths to which John West would go to get the best salmon.

And of course the most direct product humour can be extracted from the physical product itself. In our Rentlo ad, an exasperated wife tries to stir her couch potato husband from gawping at the telly by throwing the sets out of the window… only to be frustrated by Rentlo's wide screen.

Handy hint: Try reading your hysterically funny script, without mentioning the product. If it works, it's not a good ad.

9 Execution is God

How many times have you watched the first cut of your comic masterpiece, to be greeted not with a belly laugh but a belly contraction?

Oh God, it's not funny!

Or even worse, it merits that famous cop out for all failed comedy: "It's not so much a belly laugh. It's more of a wry smile."

There are only two possible conclusions that can be drawn here. Either the script wasn't as funny as you thought it was.

Or it's been badly done.

Here are a few tips from he who must be obeyed on how to avoid the latter.

The first is get the right director. It's so obvious that it hardly seems worth saying ... However, it's amazing just how often people don't.

And you have to understand one thing. Comedy is a particular talent and very few people have it. It's possible that a director, whose beautiful visual eye has accumulated more pencils than Leonardo's art bag, could be incapable of extracting even a slight titter from a whoopee cushion full of laughing gas.

And the same goes for actors and actresses. If I were asked what is the single most important thing about filming comedy, I would say casting. The set may be good, the lighting impeccable, and the special effects mind-boggling, but if the acting stinks, so will the commercial.

So don't worry about how many casting sessions you have, keep going until you ABSOLUTELY KNOW you've got the right cast.

And by all means try and find someone who looks the part. But never choose an actor or actress just because they've got a good face. (I did that once and "Sir Lawrence Olivier," as the unfortunate thesp came to be known by the crew, took what we all thought was a funny script and turned it into something about as enjoyable as a fart in a space suit.)

Remember, wardrobe and make-up can transform someone's appearance…but not their talent.

And here's a few other hints.

Most funny lines are delivered straight ... because the best jokes are usually in the eye of the beholder, not the protagonist ... and there is nothing more annoying than someone who laughs at their own jokes. (In only one XXXX script did we wrongly let the hero smile as he delivered his last line ... and it was so unfunny, we didn't run it.)

It's also why the line that gets the biggest laugh on the set is not necessarily the one that is the funniest when you come to edit it.

Because of this, I also learnt something from one of our current geniuses of comedy directing, Danny Kleinman. Always do the ending a few different ways. You think you know how it should be done but comedy, as they say, is a funny business and you never know 100%.

Oh, and on a comedy shoot, try not to trip over the cables. You're meant to write the gags, not perform them.

Handy hint: When you've handed your baby over to your chosen director, give him the space to do his job. But never forget that, when the shit hits the fan, it still is **your** *baby.*

10 Thou Shalt Keep it Dead Simple

At M&C Saatchi, our main principle is what we call the "Brutal Simplicity of Thought" because, while its easier to complicate than to simplify, simple thoughts enter the mind quicker and stay there longer. That's why the very best and most effective advertising propositions are simple.

The best ads are, at their heart, simple.

And so are the best jokes.

Here's an example from earlier in my writing career.

In the "Bridge" ad for XXXX, we showed a Ute, driven by two outbackers being driven across a bridge. In the back was the wife and about four tons of XXXX. The bridge collapsed and the wife and XXXX were left suspended over the dried up riverbed.

In the script, the wife says, "We'll be all right if we lose some weight off the back" and one of the blokes turns to his mate and says "She's not just a bloody good wife, she's a darn good sport."

As we were shooting the end, the light was disappearing rapidly and the chosen actor just could not deliver the line. By now the DOP was actually having to stick brutes through the window to light the ongoing disaster, so we had to do something quickly. In desperation we changed the actors round and I simplified the line to "She's a good sport, your missus."

One deadpan delivery later and we had a commercial that was simply 100% funnier.

Handy hint 1: Keep paring the joke down to its simplest expression… to a stage just before it becomes incomprehensible. Humour depends on people having to do a bit of work. But that work has to be rewarded.

So there we are. The 10 immutable commandments of humour.

But holy smoke! A thunderbolt has struck me in the lumbar regions. A deep voice has emanated from the fastness of the clouds and spake unto me: "Not so fast, schmuck. I feel another tablet coming on." And a finger of fire has burnt the following into the stone at my feet.

11 Thou Shalt Disobey All The Commandments Above If That Makes It Funnier

"Thou worm" spake the voice. "If thou shalt do an ad that is not simple or surprising or based on truthful observation, sex, incongruity, visual humour or any of the above encomiums and it's funny and relevant, thou shalt go with it."

"But Lord," I replied, "that's breaking the rules. And anyhow, you can't have 11 commandments."

And he spake and said unto me, "I am the God of humour. I can do whatever I bloody well like for a giggle, sunshine."

And he turned me into a planner.

THE LAW OF DISRUPTION

I f Al Ries' Positioning was probably the most influential Law of advertising in the 70s (as Simplicity and Humour perhaps were in the 60s), then Jean Marie Dru's notion of Disruption has been powerfully successful in the noughties.

His philosophy reached back to the great campaigns of VW, Nike, Apple, Heineken, among others, to look what they had in common; he realised there was always, quite literally, a before and an after — a form of change characterised by a sudden transformation in conditions.

A breakthrough, a discontinuity, a creative leap, a revolution, a "disruption."

From this analysis, Dru distilled not just a credo, but a redo, a new way to nurture great ideas, a way of thinking, a methodology. How to go about systematically generating big ideas? He called it Disruption and now his TBWA network has adopted it worldwide. Active, pregnant with opportunity, with a whiff of irreverence and creativity, it carefully harvests ideas from the emotional world of anarchy and mystery.

Conventions train us to do the conventional.

Accepted wisdoms, where everyone is thinking the same, usually means no one is really thinking; familiarity breeds inertia.

The word "disruption" is sometimes used in English, and in French, to describe a sudden opening of an electrical circuit. This image is apt. Inherent to disruption is a surge of energy. It is at once both strategy and action.

The aim of the Law of Disruption is to reframe the brand so that the market sees it differently. The brand is de-familiarised. Or re-complexified. In other words, consumers are made suddenly to see brand characteristics they had overlooked before. The result is that peoples' interest in a brand is suddenly renewed. In this way, as he writes, McDonald's is now selling fast food to the fussy French, Playstation is selling computer games to adults, and the US is buying Vodka that's not Russian.

The Law of Disruption acknowledges that having achieved a great Positioning, the battle is still not over. New attacks come all the time from competitors with new angles, and new opportunities open up in newly created spaces.

Apple's disruption, for example, overturned the conventional notion that, for high technology products, communication must revolve around product features. Steve Jobs, Apple's boss, showed that a brand "is not about bytes and boxes, it's about values."

Brands should be verbs rather than merely nouns.

Brands should stand for something (instead of everything).

Too much advertising today is satisfied with maintaining the status quo, staying within common brand imagery and me-too values. This is doomed thinking.

Advertising is at its considerable best when used as a sharp weapon. So advertise to transform the business. Make ads that go for the jugular. "Be a canon at a hare hunt," as Schopenhauer wrote.

There is no point in advertising for the status quo. Advertise for big effect. Go boldly. Play offense. Look for ads that are going to create the big dynamic.

The Law of Disruption is not about destruction, but creation. Jean Marie Dru's bestselling books, *Disruption* and *Beyond Disruption*, detail the three-stage process.

Here, in this specially created piece, he introduces some of the tools that make the Disruption so disarming.

THE LAW OF DISRUPTION BY JEAN-MARIE DRU

"Insanity is doing the same thing over and over and expecting a different result."

I wouldn't go as far as claiming that the majority of the advertising industry is crazy, but you have to admit that too many ads out there look the same and say the same, and so just get ignored.

At TBWA, we all agree that if you're going to go to the trouble to make advertising — and ask your clients to underwrite its considerable expense — then make sure it won't easily be ignored. Make sure it rewards your audience with elements of surprise and delight and the shock of recognition. Respect people's intelligence, their sense of adventure, and their wit. And while you're at it, knock them on their collective ear by revealing your clients in a whole new light. Grab unclaimed territory by showing why what your clients do is singular, extraordinary, even world-changing. And in the process, make sure your clients enjoy the stature they deserve: prominent in the culture, famous for the particular ideal they embody, and much more prosperous as a result.

We also agree that in order to do this, you can't simply rely on the creative's spark of genius. Creativity has to happen at the strategic level before the creative work begins. And what you need is BIG ideas. But how do you go about systematically generating big ideas?

We looked to the outside world for inspiration, — to history, to science, to business ... We realised that the ideas that stood out from the crowd and got noticed had fundamentally changed perception. There was a before and an after, a form of change characterised by a sudden transformation in conditions: a breakthrough, a discontinuity, a quantum leap, a revolution — a "disruption."

And what all these ideas had in common was that they had challenged the prevailing ideas of the time. Before Copernicus, the heavens rotated around the earth. Before Pasteur, there were no germs and so no immunization from them. Before Ford, automobile transportation was the luxury of a few. Each disruption changed the world, and our perception of it, utterly.

We also noticed that these ideas had all been driven by a vision. Copernicus and Pasteur already had an intuitive feeling about the theories that they went on to prove. Ford envisioned democratising automobile transportation. They all had a sense of where they were heading.

And so Disruption, the TBWA philosophy and methodology, came into being. Admittedly, Disruption sounds difficult, unsettling and fundamentally frightening. Why would anybody disrupt on purpose? The first thing to understand is that Disruption is not about destruction. It's about creation — creating something dynamic to replace something that has become static.

Disruption is not just a way to come up with advertising ideas. It's a way to think. Disruption is about systematically breaking through the barriers that shape and limit standard business approaches. It's about challenging conventional wisdom and imagining new possibilities. It's about overturning the assumptions and biases that get in the way of fresh and visionary ideas.

Disruption is the art of asking better questions in order to understand the marketplace at a much deeper level of reality, and then to use this as a strategic tool.

The Disruption Methodology – A 3-step Process

We start by identifying the conventions, the unquestioned assumptions, which shape all aspects of a company and help maintain the status quo: corporate, marketing, consumer and communication conventions.

Once we've assessed the context, we can look at how the different facets of a brand, company or category's activity fit together, and understand why things are as they are.

We then move on to the Disruption phase where we challenge the conventions in order to find the flaw in conventional thinking. Conventional assumptions create giant opportunities if you're willing to take the time to actually examine and question them. This is the

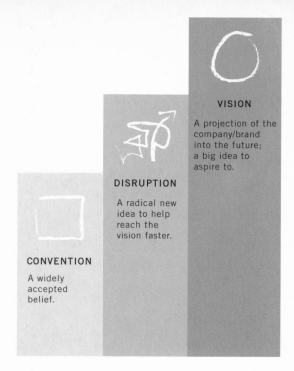

VISION

A projection of the company/brand into the future; a big idea to aspire to.

DISRUPTION

A radical new idea to help reach the vision faster.

CONVENTION

A widely accepted belief.

imaginative stage where we look for inspiring, refreshing and daring ideas to overturn the convention to the benefit of the company, an idea that defies market or category rules — a disruption.

Finally, we identify a Vision, a projection of the company or brand into the future. A vision is more than an advertising proposition or a brand positioning, it is a total culture. The vision becomes the destination against which all strategic and marketing decisions are measured. The disruptive ideas we come up with are a way to get to the vision as fast as possible.

What we're doing is taking something that sometimes happens on its own and turning it into a conscious method of generating ideas. By thinking in this way, we are able to retire low-yielding ideas and launch new, highly profitable ones. Disruption helped make PlayStation the number one game brand worldwide by appealing to a previously untapped adult audience. It demonstrated that premium vodka doesn't have to be Russian; witness the success of the iconic brand Absolut, an unknown vodka from Sweden prior to its launch in the US. And it proved that it's possible to love McDonald's, the company behind the brand, making France one of the fast food chain's most profitable markets.

Disruption: A system for People who Hate Systems

The minute you talk about methodologies, creative people get skeptical. I'm the first one to be suspicious of processes because they can be paralysing. We are looking for fresh, imaginative thinking, even in the analysis stages. As the owner and CEO of Lego said, "People who are curious, creative and imaginative — who have a childlike urge to learn — are best equipped to thrive in a challenging world and be the builders of our common future." Disruption can only be successful as a discipline if it is playful. So we have made play a discipline and our discipline playful. Childlike thinking and naïveté are encouraged. Einstein said that one of his greatest strengths was the ability to ask childlike questions. To stimulate play, we have put together a vast box of tools, available online to our 9,000 people. The box contains over 20 tools, from rainmakers for big ideas to investigative and observational analysis techniques. These tools and techniques leverage the power of fun, of theatricality.

Disruption Workshops

The most valuable disruptions occur when we are able to work hand in hand with the client who knows the ins and outs of the company better than anyone. This is why we have developed Disruption Workshops and we encourage all our clients to participate in them. There is nothing more productive than finding a disruptive idea together. The client and the agency are in total agreement, avoiding the sometimes tricky task of selling an idea to a client who has not been involved in idea generation upfront. It's a fun and rewarding exercise for both the client and the agency. Standard Bank in South Africa overhauled the entire company with a new vision and credo after participating in a Disruption Workshop. Masterfoods launched a disruptive campaign for the Whiskas brand in the US in which cats are celebrated for being cats, not pets: "Your cat has an inner beast, feed it."

Disruption and the Need for Constant Reinvention

Apple is a perfect example of a company that knows how to constantly reinvent itself by disrupting the status quo. Take the introduction of Macintosh. The convention was that people should become "computer literate," meaning that they should learn to work the way computers do. Steve Job's Disruption was: "Computers should be people literate, designed to work the way people do." The vision that computers should be at the service of mankind, and not the reverse, was aspirational and generated disruptive advertising. For 60 seconds during the 1984 Super Bowl, the famous spot entitled "1984" promised a brave new world free from the dehumanising effects of computer technology. "On January 24, 1984, Apple launches Macintosh. And you will see why 1984 won't be like 1984." The next day, 200,000 people showed up to take a look at the Macintosh. Just six hours after the unveiling, sales reached $3.5 million. The allusion to George Orwell's novel made this an unforgettable commercial. The advertising approach was as revolutionary as the product itself. With the Macintosh campaign, Apple added an advertising discontinuity to a business discontinuity.

Of course, Disruptions eventually become conventions themselves. Apple's Macintosh spurred the revolution of the PC over the monolithic mainframe. By the 1990s, PC manufacturers had caught up by developing machines that were easier to use and cheaper. This made Apple's user-friendly characteristic less of a discriminating factor. Nearly 15 years later, Apple needed to disrupt again. The "Think Different" campaign featuring great creators of the 20th century who "… are not fond of rules and have no respect for the status quo" launched Apple's new vision: Apple is a company that makes "tools for creative minds." The vision sprang from Steve Job's Disruptive conviction that the brand "is not about bytes and boxes, it's about values." The disruption overturned the convention that, for high technology products, communication must revolve around product features. The "Think Different" campaign not only re-inspired computer users, it galvanised Apple employees and heralded the introduction of the iMac, the best product expression of the newfound vision: a powerful computer with an aesthetical design (and, unlike all other computers, — colorful, not beige). The iMac also declared Apple's view of the future of computing — the floppy disk is dead. The launch of the iMac is now considered the most successful computer introduction in Apple's history, selling two million in one year.

"Think Different" would have been a great motto for the concept of Disruption.

Today, Apple is disrupting yet again with the introduction of iPod and the iTunes Music Store, allowing both Mac and PC users to legally download digital music. This is one step towards Apple's newest vision to be at the hub of the digital lifestyle. Apple never rests on its laurels, but always seeks to create new market spaces. Apple understands that you have to disrupt or be disrupted.

Great Brands Take Stands

The nirvana we're going for is a powerful vision. We work with our clients to find the strategic ideas that change the rules in their favour. Once you've done that, you can find the new path. All highly successful brands embrace a vision. They take a stand for the idea they represent. When you have a client that represents something that is their own, it's easy — well, a lot easier, anyway — to come up with intrusive campaigns that help those companies make great leaps. Our goal is to make our clients famous for the ideas they stand for, fame way beyond just having a good ad campaign. We're searching for that famous idea that can drive a company forward for many years.

Disruption is not anarchy. It is a strategically directed shake-up. It's more than a process; it's a way of thinking. It's a way to look at our client's business and find opportunity. Disruption means viewing the world with a curious, open mind. It means taking nothing for granted. It means being bold and brave. If you want your business to survive and prevail in a fast-changing world, you have to disrupt the world before the world disrupts you. The point of Disruption is simple. Invent the future so that you can own the future instead of being evicted by it.

Disrupt or be disrupted.

THE LAW OF JUMP

Originality is a boon to the advertising industry – I don't mean intrinsically, in its own right, as some kind of artistic outlet for otherwise unemployable, young creative people.

Fact is, human beings respond faster to something original. Freshness and lightness have immediacy. Immediacy is attractive.

We are hard-wired to look for "the new."

The novelty of new focuses attention. And as the first job of an ad is to get noticed (because only then will it be listened to), campaigns with truly original ideas have proved to be the most compelling of selling tools.

Originality is the wow factor.

Without a healthy dose of it, the most thoughtful strategy and worthy intentions won't get your ad up off the page. "Make it new for me," implored the poet, Ezra Pound.

In these days of utter media clutter, originality is the price of entry into people's attention span; if they've seen it before, then they'll dismiss it immediately.

The ordinary is overlooked, and the extraordinary is given a moment's glance.

"What was effective one day, for that very reason, will not be effective the next, because it has lost the maximum impact of originality," said Bill Bernbach, way back in the 1960s.

Now, some commentators are arguing that modern society is moving from the "information age" into the so-called "creative age." Brilliant. Though I can't say I've noticed a surge of originality across too many advertising markets recently. Why?

Perhaps it's still as another great American, scientist Howard Allen, observed: "Don't worry about people stealing your ideas. If your ideas are any good, you'll have to ram them down people's throats."

If so, then business leaders must change the way they think about ideas and about how their company cultures reflect that thinking. Business must cultivate a blood lust for ideas.

Easy to say, but we all know in the buttoned-up corridors of the corporate world that originality, by its nature, can be hard to appreciate in the raw.

Yet so many clients demand of their agency, "Please give me something like so and so …"

The point is, when the first "so and so" was done, there was nothing like it at all. That's likely why it worked in the first place. It was in the first place.

A truly original idea has no reference point.

If a thought is original, then there is nothing like it to easily judge it against; research is no help at the concept stage. (It was the philosopher Edmund Burke who put it succinctly: "You can't plan the future by the past.")

Which, in turn, causes another problem for us ad creators, because it means we're often asking clients to take a step into the unknown. We may have made a creative leap, but the client must also make a leap of faith.

Creativity isn't a linear process, by definition, so all the logic and cognitive analysis led to the creative brief is often of limited use. This is why, in some ways, it's even harder to buy a great idea than to have one.

Yet, in my experience, a client who has tasted the blood of a great idea usually becomes a totally different beast. "Man's mind, once stretched by a new idea, never regains its original dimensions," wrote author Oliver Wendell Holmes.

Problem is, as usual with advertising, half pregnancy. Too many advertisers try to get away with only using token originality, say, just in the filmmaking or photography or some other crafted area. This is not usually enough. To be effective, look for originality in the basic thinking. The core idea.

If it's never been done before, then that may well be reason to do it now.

Sebastian Turner has made a few successful creative leaps into original territory. For a start, he was the first to start an agency in East Germany when the Wall came down. Now that leap of faith, Scholz and Friends, is one of Europe's most awarded and regarded advertising networks.

He's also the author of a number of best selling books on advertising, one of which (Spring! in its original German title) provided the inspiration for this chapter on originality, titled "The Law of Jump!"

THE LAW OF JUMP BY SEBASTIAN TURNER

Is there a pattern behind progress?

When Columbus sailed west to get to India, when Gutenberg changed the rules of communication, when Luther challenged the Vatican, when Henry Ford revolutionised production, when Ghandi peacefully toppled the colonial power, when Konrad Zuse built the first computer, they did not take a step.

Whenever great minds change the world, they jump.

The same holds true for experiences. All great experiences are closely related to a jump.

To jump is the simple and universal principle of moving people.

The Hungarian psychologist, Mihaly Csikszentmihalyi, coined a term for the very feeling caused by a jump: He called it "flow" It is the state of mind one experiences between being bored and being frightened to death. Flow is literally the mood humans strive for.

One may call it motivation, excitement, thrill — whatever. Great communication carries people to this special point; it makes them cross a border emotionally, rationally or, at best, both.

People are also brought to this point by admen who have passed this border by themselves in the first place. All great campaigns in advertising history are based on a jump. When Bill Bernbach made Avis say "We try harder", he broke the unwritten rule that you must never allow yourself to be perceived as second. When Volkswagen asked the world to "Think small," they left behind the previously unanimous declaration that bigger is better.

To shift from stepping to jumping is not just a privilege of the titans of (advertising) history.

It is not even a privilege of an elite.

It is the behaviour of every baby that discovers the world. All you have to do is to look back at your time as a toddler, when you did dramatic things such as learning to walk, to speak, to sing and many other jumps.

Although all my professional life I have been with the same agency (no jumps there, to be honest) the start, at least, was a jump.

At 6pm on November 9,1989, I was watching CNN in my dormitory in North Carolina, when, far away, the Berlin Wall crumbled. I called Thomas Heilmann, a friend and a student of law, and we decided to make a jump. We went to East Germany to establish one of the first independent communications companies in the disappearing communist world.

No money, no professional experience, no telephone, no office, no clients — no problem, as long as there is the opportunity to jump.

Ein Sachse.

Sam Njakono Meffire.
Geboren 1970
in Zwenkau/Sachsen.

Sächsische Zeitung

Das ist Sachsen.

Xenophobic violence is countered best by courageous neighbours–such as the Saxon citizen Sam Meffire.

Our first award winning ad was published after a riot against minorities. It carried an unsurprising headline for the people in East Germany: "A Saxon." The photograph, however, was not depicting a familiar face. It showed a young man with a shaved scalp, but not a skinhead. It showed Sam Meffire, a Saxony-born civil servant whose father had been an exchange student from Africa.

The idea of the ad represents a border crossed for all involved. To the client, *Sächsische Zeitung*, the daily paper in the region, it was meant to provoke at least a small part of its audience, something a brand usually wishes to avoid. To the agency, it meant crossing the border of political advertising.

By far the largest jump, of course, was made by Sam Meffire. His calm view displayed mere courage. He knew that he would receive letters full of hate. The ad became the talk of the town and the country, Sam was invited to talk shows and could communicate his point of view to an audience much broader than the original ad, which was published just once.

Royal Air Force veteran: Let us rebuild the church.

Another notable ad involved another courageous man, Jeffrey Chapman, a veteran of the Royal Airforce and a witness of the allied air raids against the German city of Dresden in World War II.

We were looking for a person who could uniquely speak out for Anglo-German understanding. Our client, the Society to Rebuild the Church of Our Lady, was facing a discussion in the city of Dresden. Could the attempt to rebuild a church that was destroyed at the end of the war be seen as a symbol of German chauvinism?

We found Chapman after endless calls to local newspapers in England, asking for an author of a letter to the editor. We visited him and his wife in England and eventually produced an ad carrying the headline "Please help me to rebuild the church I hated to destroy."

Of course, again, this was quite a jump for an RAF veteran who had survived numerous attacks on German cities. The message was given to the local papers, who carried Chapman's message as a cover story.

An outstanding ad always tells a story that involves the jump of an individual or a group. They do something first and surprise their readers and viewers.

Ask yourself: Could your idea be considered as news? If so, you are on the right path to touch people's hearts and minds.

No subscriptions, no famous headlines. Grassroots newspaper "taz" blackmails its readers and survives.

No news! That was the story for another campaign. No news is a jump for only one industry: the media.

The grassroots paper *die tageszeitung* was desperately looking for subscribers. The paper, acclaimed for its irreverent headlines, was so broke that it could not even afford an ad campaign. However, the editor, Bascha Mika, liked to jump. It was decided to show consumers what would be missed if the paper folded. And that became a weekly event. Every week she blackmailed her readers: 300 new subscriptions were demanded by the end of the week, or the weekend edition would be published without something dear to the readers.

In most weeks more than 300 new subscribers were convinced. Occasionally, however, there were only 221 new readers, so the paper was published without any headlines. It turned out to be a collector's edition that sold particularly well.

During that one summer, more that 5,000 new subcriptions were sold, far above expectation and without one single ad placed.

Make yourself unattractive–use an insect repellent and become a relaxed frog.

Use your head and see what is there. A billboard for a hat manufacturer.

Successful communication ideas surprise people and make them think, or feel, anew. The more visual, the better.

What comes to your mind thinking about a insect repellent? Wouldn't it be great if they turned you into a frog? Depicting consumers as a frog? Pellit jumped and got an ad that stands out. A friendly, human frog wearing a tie. "Make yourself unattractive," he suggests.

A naïve look at traditional billboards columns gave birth to a campaign that uses the cliche of beauty to sell designer hats. The faces of beautiful women were placed without any addition on these columns. The artfully crafted tops of the columns all of a sudden were seen as hats.

Communication scientists have identified a model that explains the law of jump academically. Volker Trommsdorff, former president of the German Society of Advertising Science (one is not really surprised to find an institution like this in Germany) and noted marketing scholar, defined two contradictory effects in creative communication.

The effect of motivation is juxtaposed by the effect of difficulty. No difficulty means no motivation, just indifference.

Too much difficulty, however, causes confusion.

The art of communication is to jump far enough that people get involved and still get the point — the optimum (see graph).

Nice place. But have you ever been to the State of Baden-Württemberg? Take the train!

Can advertisers jump too far? Yes, but it rarely happens. Compared with the bulk of advertising, which is both boring and unforgettable, cases of confusion seem negligible. Imagine standing on a railway platform in – let's say Berlin, and a locomotive slowly passes by. Nothing motivating, yet. Imagine, however, that the train carries an ad saying "Not too bad — But have you ever been to the State of Baden-Württemberg?"

This is how the federal state in southwestern Germany appealed to travellers. The lord mayor of Frankfurt got the message. She ordered that the Frankfurt buses were not allowed to carry the ad any longer. Thank you for making the Baden-Württemberg buses move even more people.

You are not handicapped.

Every Mercedes is built to make driving easier for people with disabilities.   Mercedes-Benz

A symbol is what you make out of it.

By altering a well-known symbol just a little bit, Mercedes-Benz caught the eye of a very small target group. The official sign for handicapped puts a wheel under the sitting individual. The ad turns it into a steering wheel and advertises "You are not handicapped," as long as you drive a specially equipped Mercedes.

Mercedes crossed the border in using a symbol many mainstream brands would not dare to touch. And they were applauded by the handicapped for bringing their issue to a broader audience.

Another group that receives anything but public recognition are the drivers of heavy trucks. They slow down traffic and cause jams. So wouldn't the best ad space be billboards at traffic hot spots? Almost. The very best space is the of the truck. It allows the driver a small conversation about his job and his contribution to society in general and the driver behind in particular.

Mercedes-Benz offered truckers giant stickers to cover the back of their lorries. The headlines are friendly explanations that everyone understands: "As long as sausage cannot be sent by e-mail, we have the share the road,"

And, "Of course I am slower than you. I am carrying your red wine home."

Again, something new was done and received wide attention. Over 1,000 trucks are continuing their participation two years after the initiative was launched.

Stuck in a jam? Blocked by a truck? Listen and love the guy who is carrying your red wine, sausage and newspapers. Rolling billboards for Mercedes-Benz commercial vehicles.

For the sister brand of Mercedes, the tiny smart cars, the conventional wisdom of brochures was put aside. Smart cars are so small that two can easily park in the space required by a regular car. This inspired the unique design for a brochure. The regular format can be separated into two smaller, identical brochures. One to keep, one to give away to a friend.

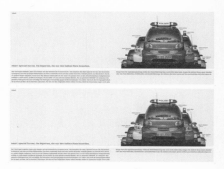

Two smart cars fill one regular parking space. Thus, two smart brochures fit into one regular brochure. One is for your friend.

The campaign for *Frankfurter Allgemeine Zeitung* violates everything one may have learned in art school about celebrity campaigns. A campaign that jumps right at the optimum spot of perception breaks the rule of testimonial advertising and can involve heads of government, world renowned writers, artists and celebrities.

The celebrities are not seen. A small printed headline reads "There is always a clever mind behind it." Super model Nadja Auermann, movie director Billy Wilder, statesman Helmut Kohl and the like were asked to pose for a photograph that covers their face with a newspaper! The viewers of the ad are invited to guess who is hidden. Only a small by-line uncovers the secret. Among giraffes, the long-legged beauty Nadja is reading, in the middle of the Hollywood sign Billy Wilder reads, Cardinal Karl Lehmann reads in a flock of sheep, and on a giant ship named *Europe* the champion of European Union, Helmut Kohl, takes a break and reads the paper.

The campaign received more free media than paid-for ad space. It made headline news over and over. Museums are collecting it, and the circulation of the paper has surpassed 400,000 copies for the first time.

There is always a clever mind behind this newspaper. Supermodel Nadja Auermann among long-legged Giraffes.

Hollywood sign? Read again. It's the Billy-Wilder-Sign

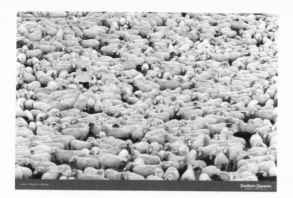

Cardinal Karl Lehmann reads the paper in a flock of sheep.

The man who made Europe move: German statesman Helmut Kohl aboard "Europe."

One of Germany's most talked about ads features the CEO of Deutsche Bank, Hilmar Kopper. In a press conference, he made a remark that has haunted him ever since. In a giant real estate break up, he called the unpaid bills of some handymen "peanuts." An outcry rocked the media. Isn't this evidence of the cold arrogance of corporate fat cats?

Listening to a speech of his on banking issues, an idea came to my mind. Why not ask him to participate in a campaign. The picture: He is sitting on a mountain of peanuts. Mr. Kopper showed good humour. When approached he laughed and said: "Why not?"

Germany's foremost banker sitting on a mountain of peanuts. His critics are disarmed by his sense of humour.

As soon as his schedule coincided with the peanut harvest, a picture was taken in Georgia (close to Plaines, by the way). A symbol of corporate power pokes fun at himself, bringing his own gaffe into an advertising picture. Kopper made a giant jump hardly anyone had expected, possible for a top executive from one of the largest banks in the world.

Through this unexpected ad, he turned his image around. Even his hardest critics, the media, heralded his sense of humour and shed a friendly light on the banker.

The law of jump involves everybody: the creatives, strategists, clients, celebrities, the media and, of course, the public. It's easy to apply.

You'll know when you've crossed the line from stepping to jumping. Your audience will, too.

Jump and enjoy!

THE LAW OF FASCINATION

There's an old Arab caravanserai superstition that says, "Never count your camels, in case one dies."

No, I don't understand it either.

But neither do I understand the superstitious forces that make marketers congregate around the same positionings. No doubt, it's also some strange herding instinct.

"Give me something like that," they cry, believing that doing what another has done before gives it a magic power to work again. Unfortunately, because the original idea was probably not "just like" anything, but successfully "unlike anything else," this theory breaks down. What made the original idea work in the first place was that it was "in the first place."

What is this weird funnelling effect that draws marketers to the "me too"; a black hole inviting parity; me-too mania; cloned thinking; is there a Bermuda Triangle-like pull towards what's been done in the past?

When will marketers learn that category-style imagery is simply of benefit to the category leader? I'm reminded of that famous scene in the Monty

Python film *Life of Brian,* where the faithful crowd chant in unison: "We're all individuals!"

The mind-numbing sameness of the category screenings of work entered in the Cannes Festival is stunning; mind you, that's exactly how many consumers feel. Problem is, you can't sell to anyone asleep.

We live in a world full of extraordinary things. To stand out as a mere advertising idea, you simply must be outstanding.

The Law of Fascination demands a more positive and proactive attitude to advertising. People now buy in repertoires. This is not where smart marketers want their brands to be.

This tendency towards sameness in advertising, as opposed to basic differentiation, has inspired the following discussion of two types of advertising: the convergence theory of advertising versus the conquest theory. Or the weak theory versus the strong.

Our next jurist is Reg Bryson, 20 years CEO of Australia's The Campaign Palace, who studied at Harvard. He nominates the Law of Fascination. Bryson urges that we resist the race to converge in the one ideal position. Even the highest performing companies regress to the industry mean in three to seven years, as he points out.

Evolution shows that the race to the best positioning is actually not about the survival of the fittest. But who is fittest to adapt.

Ask any camel.

THE LAW OF FASCINATION BY REG BRYSON

Why Advertising Isn't Working

It would be more than fair to suggest that the advertising industry has been low on many of the vital signs over the past decade. As an industry, it lacks the ring of confidence and its stocks of conviction are low. One reason for this low state is that the advertising industry may have been wrongly convinced of exactly what advertising is capable of.

Put simply, there are two schools of thought on how advertising works: **the "strong" theory** — that advertising is indeed persuasive — and **the "weak" theory** — that advertising's key role is one of reinforcement and reminder. It's obvious that the more commonly held theory today is the "weak force" rationalist's view that advertising's primary role is that of maintaining or reinforcing a brand's salience among consumers.[1]

We are told that advertising is, at best, a supporter of other, more direct marketing activities and a reinforcer of existing attitudes, values and predispositions. The trouble with this passive, "preach to the converted" approach is that few consumers are indeed converted. Brand loyalty in most markets is a misnomer. In category after category, consumers are purchasing across a repertoire of brands they perceive to be more similar than dissimilar. The missionary zeal of marketing activity and branding of past decades simply isn't paying off. In the minds of many, advertising is not paying its way.

Brands, the cornerstone concept of modern marketing practice, have reached a crisis point of commodification — no differentiation, no loyalty and no impact. It seems strange that the vast number of marketers who both subscribe to and practice this reinforcement theory don't realise that if advertising is indeed a weak force, then it gets weaker still as a brand matures and consumers become more familiar with it.[2] Too many of today's advertisers seem content simply to follow the crowd. Too many businesses are simply going from A to B, following the well-trodden, conventional business path.

In any business, in any industry, in any area, there's a gravity trap — a strong force field that pulls you back to the mean, back to industry sameness. Far too many companies have gravitated into the trap of marketing convention. With this comes conventional practices, conventional approaches, conventional thinking, conventional strategies, conventional research leading to conventional advertising.

Convergence Advertising

This trend towards "same sameness" is having a profoundly depressing effect on advertising worldwide. No one is challenging preconceived notions. Creative advertising is becoming an oxymoron! The fact is,

---

[1] Andrew Ehrenberg, *Justifying Advertising Budgets*, Admap, South Bank University, UK, 1997.

[2] Conclusion from Vakratsas and Ambler LBS Study.

following conventional wisdom in any industry has the effect of homogenising competition.

Fact: "Me too" strategies rarely work.

Fact: Advantage does not come from imitation.

The extent and serious effect this commercially crippling convergence force actually has on a corporation is not widely known. A McKinsey[3] study of 400 companies over 30 years found that even high-performing companies regress to the industry mean in three to seven years.

Recent Prestige car advertising — seven different makes, eight different models, similar ad small car manufacturers — All targeting the "Red Seeking Single Page Reading" audience's Convergence of Concept and Medium. These were the first five ads to appear in *She Magazine,* July 1998 issue.

Twenty years ago, there was a lot of difference in brands, in products and in advertising.

---

[3] David Yoffie,Harvard Business School 1998.

A key imperative of the "branding" approach was deliberate management action to combat the natural tendency towards commodification.

What Happened to Differentiation?

Research indicates[4] that consumers see most brands in a category as more or less the same. The manufacturers or brand owners obviously see things differently. They see their brands as trustmarks that have stood the test of time, that stand for quality, value, familiarity, confidence, reassurance, integrity.

Advertising is used to place their brand on a pedestal, to give their product *at least* a sense of brand presence (if not a sense of grandeur); a presence that influences and informs the ever-receptive respondent that a purchase decision in favour of this brand would indeed be an astute and easy decision.

Inherent in this philosophy is that consistency and credentials are more important than creativity. Also, there is a higher need for recognition and awareness than for consumer interest and involvement. This is the kind of advertising that is defended, especially by major corporations and their agencies, as being "good, solid advertising".

Why would a brand owner challenge this approach?

The advertising appropriately celebrates the product and, besides, it must be right, everyone's doing it! This indeed is the kind of advertising that keeps a client happy! Michael Porter, the Harvard marketing guru, once claimed that "strategy is the race to the one ideal position." There is a problem if everyone gets there at around the same time.

Differentiation, however, remains a critical aspect of marketing. Yet, as the examples above well illustrate, convergence not differentiation is currently the defining force.

Despite what you may believe as a brand owner, it's little wonder that consumers believe brands are look-alikes, act-alikes, do-alikes: brands that stand for nothing in particular and everything in general. This obviously leads to eeny-meeny-miny-mo decision-making and this obviously leads to purchasing across a repertoire of brands and this obviously is exactly what consumers are currently doing in category after category.

---

[4] Ehrenberg *op cit.*

Brand Parity Has Become, Through Bland Advertising, Bland Parity

We've seen the commodification of brands, with no differentiation and no loyalty. Brands are becoming generic. We've seen the commodification of advertising, with nothing fresh, nothing rewarding, nothing distinguishing. Unfortunately for the industry, we've also seen, in the eyes of many clients, the commodification of agencies. Clients appropriately hold the perception that "you can get ads from anybody."

Creativity in advertising is now more about processing and packaging than about uniqueness or creating differentiation. Advertising is now more about deference and discounting than courage and conviction.

The Danger of Safety

A safe brand idea or advertising idea is actually dangerous because it can delude the company buying it into thinking it will work for them. In a cluttered environment, however, driven by hyper-competition, brand names or advertising ideas that merely fit are lost. Great brand ideas should frighten you when you first see them, because if they don't, they haven't got the power to compete.

Despite what conventional wisdom would have you believe, there is much greater risk in the conventional, the comfortable, the conservative approach than in a fresh, unique, differentiated — dare we say? — "creative" approach. Agencies are pursuing safety-first advertising solutions to satisfy the client rather than reward the consumer.

Many clients currently feel secure only with ongoing reinventions of advertising that has worked in the past. Additionally, risk-averse clients are not being challenged by defensive, inward-looking agencies. To quote Gary Moss from his days at Campbells: "The problem is that agencies are so skittish now about how the client is going to react to something that they are thinking and acting like the client and once the agency becomes the client we don't need them anymore."

We are left with a situation where neither agency nor marketing department believes it can afford to take risks. All this is producing advertising that is falling in value as a business investment because its consumer focus is wavering.

Indeed, few marketers have actually considered the high cost of convergence. A US study[5] found with ads reflecting the category style that for every $9 spent, $5 goes to the brand and $4 goes to the category leader. The sum of all this is that conventionality carries a long list of risks and a shortage of reward: the risk of not being noticed; the risk of not being remembered; the risk of being undifferentiated; the risk of being confused with competitors saying the same thing and looking the same; the risk of not carving out for the brand a distinctive brand stance and personality; the risk of boring consumers rather than stimulating them; the risk of using your company's hard-earned dollars to subsidise the competition.

It appears that attempts at advertising "safety" seem to achieve more harm than good. There are indications that insecure marketers will find the industry convention "safety" route less easy to defend in the future.

Our industry's equivalent of "no one ever got fired for buying IBM" may soon be put to the test. A recent survey[6] found that only 20% of CEOs are happy with the current marketing process or believe it is making an effective contribution to shareholder value. Of the CEOs surveyed, 65% claimed they will reassess the role of marketing.

Marketing has moved, in little more than a decade, from being the bees-knees department, where achievements were measured in milestones, to a department where progress and impact is now being measured by the millimeter. Marketing simply isn't moving people the way it used to. And advertising, applied in this way, is no longer paying its way.

Why Advertising is Your Most Potent Weapon

It's been said that advertising that significantly disturbs the status quo in a market is remarkably rare. Advertising achieves its role most successfully by being creative.[7] Creativity, however, appears to be hardly discussed these days, let alone valued, understood, sought after or applied. It seems companies don't currently hold high expectations of advertising. It seems they'd rather "fit in" than "be famous." The old ideal that "good is the enemy of the great" has lost out to "close enough is good enough" and "quick enough is better." It appears these

---

[5] Millward Brown, USA.

[6] Survey of 25% of CEOs of Australia's Top 1,000 companies, Centre of Applied Marketing, UNSW, and Stratos Consulting, 1998.

[7] "Are We All Barking Up the Wrong Trees", *Brand Values*, Admap, U.K., May 1998.

days that there is limited support for the view that advertising is a potent, powerful, persuasive force capable of transforming a company's business

However, there are a number of global spirits who would argue that maintaining the weak approach in this day and age is nothing short of commercial stupidity. There are people who truly believe that doing the forgettable is unforgivable. The true believers in the opposite camp to the reinforcement school believe that advertising is persuasive, that it can change attitudes, that it can change behaviour, that it doesn't merely influence sales but can, indeed, create sales.

Advertising should not be regarded or used simply as a passive tool. It must be an active weapon. It must do something. It must have an effect.

Well used, great advertising can be the last legal means of gaining an unfair advantage over your competition. It's very difficult in today's competitive environment to have a significant product advantage. It's very difficult in today's competitive environment to have a marketing budget that's significantly greater than your competition. It's very difficult in today's competitive environment to have a demonstrably better distribution system than your competition. It's very difficult in today's competitive environment to have a superior price advantage over your competition. However, through your approach to advertising you can have an unfair advantage over your competition. Albert Einstein postulates "Logic will take you from A to B ... imagination will take you everywhere."

A company should have huge ambition for the effect of its advertising. An agency must also hold huge ambition for the clients it works with — ambition that drives it beyond the supposedly safe standard solutions. Clearly, newness is needed: a new way of looking at things; a new approach.

Conquest Advertising

Strategically and creatively, advertising has to offer more, do more and deliver more. We can no longer compete by being conventionally competitive; competition is essential for survival, but no longer sufficient for success. What is required now is *brand separation*.

The conquest approach recognises that the future health of a brand is not about brand competitiveness; it's about *brand distancing*. It's about creating space around a brand — lots of space. What else does the conquest approach hold high? Conquest advertising recognises that it's a guest in the home and a guest in the mind. Conquest advertising gets talked about, becomes part of the language and achieves social currency.

The conquest approach understands that people appreciate cleverness. A clever ad equates to a clever product made by a clever company. Conquest advertising recognises that similarity and familiarity breed apathy — safety doesn't work anymore. Only the wonderful works.

Conquest advertising costs much less than dull, unimaginative convergence advertising. The conquest approach does not need a media barrage to cut through. It's finesse not force. It's a knockout punch, not 15 rounds of bombardment. It's brains not muscle.

The Critical Differentiator

There exists a volume of proof that consumers don't see brands with great advertising as more or less the same as other brands in the category. They think and feel differently about brands with great advertising — they genuinely like brands with great advertising. They see these brands as unique and differentiated from their competitors.

As outlined earlier, most companies see their brands as trustmarks that have stood the test of time; that stand for quality, value, familiarity; that exude confidence, reassurance and integrity.

As hard won as these attributes are, the trouble is that they are simply no longer enough. For example, there are at least five brands of tomato sauce available on the supermarket shelf that all reflect all of these attributes — Heinz, Rosella, Watties, IXL, Fountain. Additionally, in spite of the length of tenure and the long, long marketing history of each of these brands, how do you distinguish between them? Where are the areas of future differentiation?

Familiarity always equates to favourability, but all five are familiar! Gary Hamel said, "Once a brand starts to be referred to as 'good old XYZ', beware; it's a short step from affectionate to old fashioned!" Which of these five are seen to be old fashioned? Which of these five has a degree of contemporary emotional attachment?

Differentiation is critical. It is important at the birth of the brand and needs to be kept important, and fresh, right throughout the entire life of the brand. Brand knowledge accumulates as memories[8] and needs to be refreshed with new news.

---

[8] D. Vakratsas and T. Ambler, *Advertising Effects, A Taxonomy And Review Of Concepts, Methods & Results From Academic Literature*, Marketing Science Institute, Cambridge, Ma: 1992.

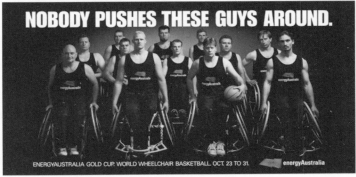

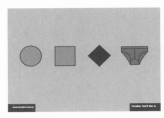

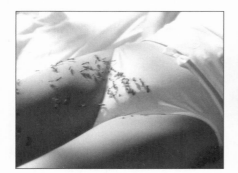

We know that behaviour is driven by memories. It has also been shown that affect is more important for decision-making than cognition.[9] (Affective memory = feelings and emotions. Cognition = knowledge and awareness.)

Over the past few years a number of new theories have drawn on advances in neurobiology, including the role of emotions, and how memory works. They all suggest that the rational persuasion approach should at least be challenged, if not abandoned. What is most important is whether advertising stimulates an emotional response from the consumer. Behavioural changes flow from the emotional engagement with the brand, not from "rational" conscious engagement.

Another truly surprising but little-known recent finding that supports this point of view comes from the work of Daniel Kahneman of Princeton who, in 2002, was awarded the Nobel Prize for *Economics*. His work, for the first time, recognised and admitted that it's the power of emotions and a person's psychological makeup that are the key determining factors in buying behaviour.

The feelings and emotional memories instilled and left by advertising can be powerful. Conquest advertising is one of the very few potent weapons that can alter memory, influence attitudes, change minds and change behaviour.

Perhaps the key outcome of conquest advertising as a differentiator is as a relationship developer. The key role of advertising now is less about selling and more about building a relationship with consumers in a clever, charming, honest, fascinating and, importantly, likeable way — helping the buyers buy, rather than simply helping the sellers sell.

Advertising that treats the consumer with intelligence, respect and with the familiarity of a good friend builds a fund of benevolence, an emotional bank balance that is traded or withdrawn from at the point of purchase.

JP Jones, an advocate of the persuasion model of advertising, concluded in a recent study that the most successful campaigns were not "hard selling" but instead were likeable, rewarding the viewer by being entertaining or amusing and said something important about the brand.[10]

---

[9] AR Damasio – *Descartes' Error: Emotion, Reason and the Human Brain*, London: Macmillan, 1994.

[10] JP Jones, Is Advertising Still Salesmanship?, *Journal of Advertising Research U.S.A.*, 37.3, 1998.

Consumers are not interested in brands or companies who have nothing better to talk about but themselves. *If a company advertises in a dull, boring and expected manner, then the company is perceived as dull, boring and unexciting.* If advertising talks down, insults the intelligence or patronises, it is perceived as misanthropic and turns the consumer away from the brand and company.

Today's marketing- and advertising-literate consumers know what we're trying to do to them and usually see through the clumsy attempts to influence them of companies which are not consumer-literate. Researcher Hugh Mackay recently commented: "Australians are tired of too much rationality, too much reasonableness ... too much dullness. Australians are yearning for more passion in their lives.

"Successful brands will be those that exhibit vitality, energy, passion and confidence ... they want to be swept away."

Brand marketing in the new millennium is not a battle of products, it's a battle of perceptions, and the management and development of brand perceptions is the management and development of consumer perceptions.

Conquest advertising actively and intentionally sets out to win friends. *Like it or not, likeability must now be considered a critical component of brand marketing.*

New research[11] into how the brain works, indicates the first response to a stimulus is an emotional one which precedes any rational response. Without a suitable emotional response, the message will not pass onto the conscious brain. If your brand reaches that brain in a fresh and memorable way, then you stand a very good chance of being remembered fondly where it counts the most.

Creativity is a potent weapon to help you shape the game you play, to help you achieve differentiation from competitors and brand dominance in the hearts and minds of consumers.

We know differentiation works.

An analysis of 55 US corporations[12] found that brands that grew differentiation between 1993 and 1995 also grew operating profits significantly more than brands that failed to grow differentiation, and more than brands that merely increased salience.

We know creativity works, that likeability works.

---

[11] Du Pleiss, *Advertising Likeability*, Admap, UK, October 1998.

[12] Y&R Study of 55 publicly traded US corporations, Admap UK, 1998.

A two-year study into the effectiveness of acclaimed commercials[13] found that awarded ads were, on average, at least 2.5 times more effective than average commercials.

We know great advertising does indeed create sales.

The first year of the Red Meat "Feel Good" campaign contributed incremental revenue of almost $1 billion to the industry.

We also know creativity is not an end in itself. It's simply a business tool — no more, no less. The fact that a concept has more impact, is more inventive, stimulating, involving, memorable, informative, charming, compelling, persuasive, captivating, likeable and talked about is not entirely the point. The point is that the more of these values you have in your advertising, the more effective you are.

At the Harvard Business School, the starting point of the process of brand building is summarised in two words:

"Be fascinating".

Enough said.

---

[13] Donald Gunn, Leo Burnett Chicago, Two-year study of the 200 most awarded commercials in the world, 1992–93.

THE LAW OF
IRREVERENCE

*T*he *G Spot Café answers their phone with
"hello," so the caller has to ask, "Is that the
G'Spot?"
The response is: "Oh, yes, yes, my God,
you've found it."*

Advertising is an expensive business. That's why
the Crime of Being Earnest is so common. So much
is at stake, it's hard to stay loose.

Yet, spend a few moments before you waste
your money and watch people flicking across TV
channels or flipping through a magazine; you soon
realise that unless you first stop people in their tracks,
you'll never get around to delivering your message.

Shock treatment is an answer. But unless your
shock is relevant to the product, then it is pointless
and dismissed by the audience.

This is where a little irreverence is a good thing.
It provides a mild surprise, a spark of life, among all
the deathly try-hards, with a pleasing lack of pretension.
Advertising festivals are full of wonderful examples
of irreverent success. Award juries are clearly attracted
to chutzpah; they reward ads that are cheeky and
roguish.

It's the same with real people; they love a bit of knowing naughtiness — otherwise the rock'n'roll industry may never have gotten started. Yet, wherever you look, mainstream advertising, whether you're in the US, UK, EEC or Southeast Asia, is numbingly PC.

Major brands talk about having character and personality, yet they're more dully politically correct than even the most colourless real person. This is an opportunity that hasn't escaped marketers with youth products. A brand is a badge of honour for teenagers even if more sensible and mature folk disapprove of something they buy. Same with its advertising. Risqué is cool, particularly if only the prime target audience "gets it."

The Cannes award-winning print ad from a couple of years ago, where the erect nipples of a bratty young couple gawking for the photo were in the exact shape of the Playstation's control teats, is one example.

Years ago, I remember a notorious magazine called *OZ* sought to do the most irreverent ads they could possibly conceive: one, for the Formal Wear Hire Company, showed a news photo of a Buddhist monk in the act of self-immolation, with the headline:

He's warm, but is he well dressed?

More recently, the Church of England in Birmingham, England, ran a poster campaign showing the crucifixion with the headline: "Body piercing? Jesus had his done 2,000 years ago." The Anglican high churchman, defending the campaign, said: "Anything that makes impact on the close up world is of value."

Damn right!

Irreverence works in many categories, not just because it can be provoking, but also because it is *real*. Satire works in communication because it taps into (healthy) scepticism among consumers about the sincerity of advertising and brands. Ads honest enough to admit that most people don't believe ads — like the old Joe Isuzu campaign — stand out because of it.

In South America, the rampant kidnapping industry is a reality, so some irreverent advertisers have even successfully played on that. One campaign recently showed a businessman being snatched off the street, subdued not by chloroform or guns, rather by the incredibly comfortable and sleep-making mattress the advertiser was promoting.

Too much advertising is too glib, too far removed from the laughable reality that everyday people cope with. So create advertising around the way real people talk, not the way other advertising people write — greasy, slick and old-fashioned. Irreverence cuts ice because it demonstrates real humanity. It says: "We are one of you, not one of them."

Monty Python comedian, John Cleese, once noted: "You usually find that it's the thing that a small number of people object to that makes the large number of people laugh the most."

While the examples I've quoted above may seem shocking and totally inappropriate for mainstream commercialism, don't forget that, in their day, mainstream phenomena like the Beatles, Madonna and Shakespeare were considered irreverent. When it comes to success, *Forbes* magazine's editor, Peter Kafka, talking about the rating in Forbes Top 100 celebrities list in 2003, commented: "Good press, bad press, all press is equal in our eyes." Be provocative. Be unafraid. Because, as Bill Bernbach noted, there is practically nothing that is not capable of boring us.

Australian-born advertising author, cutting-edge writer, and former creative director, Jim Aitchison, lives, lectures and broadcasts in Southeast Asia, where advertising is often strait-laced by government decree — yet the wonderful citizens there fairly bubble with untidy humanity.

Here, he calculates the commercial virtues of a sense of naughtiness.

THE LAW OF IRREVERENCE BY JIM AITCHISON

The second-greatest television commercial ever made, as voted in viewer polls and based on the collective opinion of the American marketing communications industry, is highly irreverent. When it was first screened in 1969, it certainly raised eyebrows as well as sales. And even by today's more liberal standards, it remains fresh and challenges convention.

The commercial is Volkswagen's *Funeral*. The brief had been prosaic enough: communicate the economy of owning a Volkswagen. The solution: a funeral cortege of expensive limousines tailed by a sobbing young man in a lone VW Beetle. The voice of the deceased, a rich old miser, intones the provisions of his Will as each beneficiary is seen riding in his or her limo. "To my wife, Rose, who spent money like there was no tomorrow, I leave one hundred dollars … and a calendar. To my sons, Rodney and Victor, who spent every dime I ever gave them on fancy cars and fast women, I leave fifty dollars … in dimes. To my business partner, Jules, whose only motto was 'Spend! Spend! Spend!' … I leave Nothing! Nothing! Nothing!" At last we reach the young man in the VW. "Finally, to my nephew Harold, who oft-times said, 'A penny saved is a penny earned,' and who also oft-times said, 'Gee, Uncle Max, it sure pays to own a Volkswagen,'" I leave my entire fortune of one hundred billion dollars."

It was the first time an American TV commercial had lampooned death and funerals. Its creator, the legendary art director, Roy Grace, then at Doyle Dane Bernbach New York, is a staunch believer that any ingredient of irreverence in communications really makes people pay attention, wins their favour and amuses them. "Everyone likes to see you take a poke at the establishment," he chuckled when I met him. As Roy recalled ironically, the client's brother had died just before the "*Funeral*" storyboard was presented. Fortunately for Roy Grace, and millions of viewers, the client was not influenced by personal considerations.

Why is irreverence so important? Simply because it's one thing to be funny, but another matter entirely to create an enduring piece of communication. Mostly, humour alone is not enough. A bare joke wears thin after repeated viewings. Humour needs an edge.

Irreverence invests a commercial with a very different quality. Irreverence has the potential to make the ad an icon, to enter the public consciousness and remain there long after the commercial has finished playing. (Significantly VW *Funeral* was voted into second

VW "Funeral"

1 I, Max E. Mably, being of sound mind and body, do hereby bequeath the following:

2 To my wife, Rose, who spent money like there was no tomorrow, I leave 100 dollars and a calendar.

3 To my sons, Rodney and Victor, who spent every dime I ever gave them on fancy cars and fast women, I leave 50 dollars in dimes.

4 To my business partner, Jules, whose only motto was "Spend! Spend! Spend!" I leave Nothing! Nothing! Nothing!

5 Finally, to my nephew, Harold, who ofttimes said, "a penny saved is a penny earned," and who also ofttimes said, "Gee, Uncle Max, it sure pays to own a Volkswagen," I leave my entire fortune of 100 billion dollars.

6

place in 2000, 30 years after it had first run. The commercial voted into first place, Apple's *1984*, arguably also contained a big dose of irreverence, certainly towards IBM!) Simply put, despite all the "funny" ads made since 1969, nothing better had come along. VW *Funeral* remained a defining moment in television advertising.

Irreverence can be applied in four ways:
- Lampoon the client and product
- Lampoon people that people love to hate (rude hotel employees, for example)
- Lampoon the establishment (lawyers, politicians, the police, officialdom and authority figures)
- Lampoon the human condition, including death.

Lampooning the client and the product calls for a certain bravery, admittedly, but it's very sound strategically and psychologically. We all rather like people who can tell a joke against themselves. We'd like to spend time with them, have a drink with them. Self-depreciating humour signals they don't take themselves so seriously because they're confident of themselves, and comfortable with who they are. They don't resort to pomposity. In the hands of Bill Bernbach, Helmut Krone and Roy Grace, Volkswagen engaged in many classic executions of the notion that VW is "ugly but it works."

Another master of this genre was a Sydney used-car dealer Ron Hodgson, a major TV advertiser in the 1970s. While his competitors desperately tried to communicate sincerity and integrity, Hodgson pioneered politically incorrect humour with himself as the butt of the joke. One memorable commercial featured British comedian Warren Mitchell in his Alf Garnett character, challenging the honesty of the client. ("You believe that, mate, you'd believe anything…") Hodgson clearly recognized the fact that he had to work harder to win the trust of cynical viewers, and he won it through irreverence.

Lampooning people we love to hate is very satisfying and disarming. Roy Grace employed this form of irreverence when he made the famous American Tourister commercial where a gorilla hurls a suitcase around in a cage, smashing it against the bars and stomping on it. The voice-over addressed not the consumer but, rather, those who would handle the consumer's luggage: "Dear clumsy bellboys, brutal cab drivers, careless doormen, ruthless porters, and all butterfingered luggage handlers all over the world, have we got a suitcase for you …" It was irreverence that truly resonated!

If the connection with the brand is appropriate, then lampooning the establishment wins lots of friends. For example, Saatchi & Saatchi Wellington satirised politicians. In their delightful commercial, a politician canvasses for votes door-to-door and is offered a piece of Whittaker's "Good Honest" chocolate. Immediately after he takes a bite, he tells the truth. "As your MP, I'll be abusing the free airfares, as will my wife and my mistress … I'll go joyriding in government limos … I'll spend a lot of time in bars, massage parlors …"

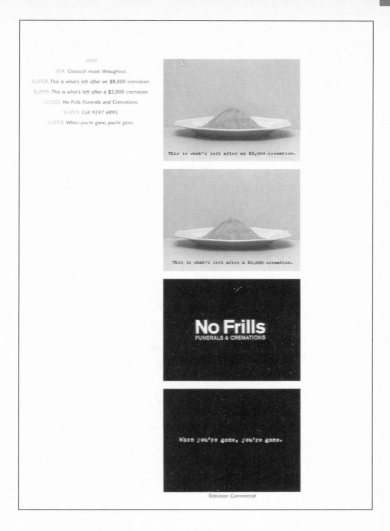

Television Commercial

Lowe & Partners India went even further in their campaign for *The Times of India*. Demonstrating how well the newspaper understood the Indian ethos, they satirised money-minded cricketers who endorsed a barrage of products. Next, they bravely satirised India's corrupt bureaucracy: an old man, trying to lodge his papers at a government department, is shunted from one shabby desk to another in a sped-up, hand-held parody of a hockey match.

Irreverence directed at the human condition is enormously powerful. Cliff Freeman & Partners New York have tilted at windmills

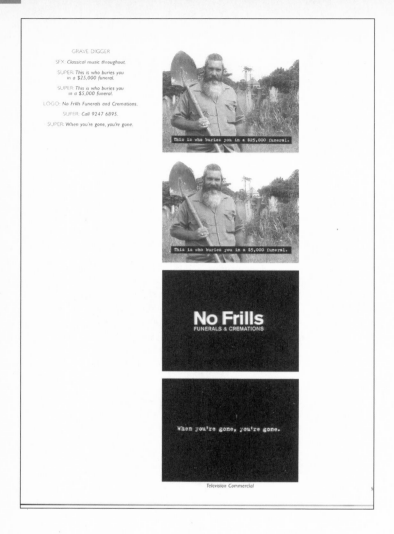

Television Commercial

for clients such as Little Caesars Pizza. They lampooned babies and hospitals. Even that sacred cow called death did not escape. To promote the movie *The Minus Man*, Freeman showed two young adults so engrossed in talking about the movie that the girl ran late for her job. By the time she had sprinted to where she worked, she discovered two elderly people floating face down in an indoor swimming pool. Only then do we realise that she was supposed to be the lifeguard.

American Tourister "Gorilla"

1 Dear clumsy bellboys . . .

2 . . . brutal cab drivers . . .

3 . . . careless doormen . . .

4 . . . ruthless porters . . .

5 . . . and all butterfingered luggage handlers all over the world . . .

6 . . . have we got a suitcase for you.

Saatchi & Saatchi Sydney (under the creative direction of this project's originator, Michael Newman) applied grim irreverence for client No Frills Funerals. The whole sentiment of the campaign was "When you're gone, you're gone." One commercial contained a black screen throughout. The first caption appeared with the message: "This is what it looks like to be buried in a $25,000 funeral." Retaining the black screen, the next caption observed: "This is what it looks like to be buried in a $5,000 funeral."

The golden rule is to make sure your irreverence isn't irrelevant. The gorilla was relevant to the strength of the suitcase. The funeral was a parallel world to cars (it would not have worked so well for a product like chewing gum, for instance) and a miser's funeral was relevant to the economy of owning a Volkswagen. Being "good honest" chocolate was all about the truth. No Frills was all about no frills and being thrifty. And so it goes.

In this age of cynical, disbelieving viewers, irreverence lets a message bond better with the audience. Audiences are all too ready to laugh *at* advertisers, and mostly with good reason. If we can accept that reality, smart marketers should factor irreverence into their communications and make the brand-consumer conversation more real and more rewarding.

THE LAW OF TASTE

The customer is king. Except in many agency creative departments, where winning awards turns you into royalty. The customer is king. Except in many agency network boardrooms, where winning new business rules.

The customer is king.

Except in many client hierarchies, where advertising standards reflect what junior managers believe will get the nod of approval later when they present the work to their senior people.

So, perhaps the customer has been dethroned.

In fact, maybe the customer's interests are more often king-hit. I recall a senior FMCG marketer once rejecting a TVC script by explaining: "the problem is, that idea is only made for the market!"

I recall another large manufacturer admitting that he ran national TV campaigns to "educate the sales force."

The customer is about third in line, at best.

And what's the result? Hobbled marketing. Advertising as a dull and blunted instrument. Oh yes, and customers in a right royal fug.

Whatever else, surely the focus of the marketing effort must be on the person that the ads are talking to? Too many campaigns are pretending to address the market, but are continually looking over their shoulder and around the room for nods of approval.

There are even award winning campaigns that are simple, humorous and fascinating, obeying any number of the Laws in this book, but these ads may still be unsuccessful in the marketplace.

Because, for one reason or the other, many campaigns are not truly aimed at the end user; whether they're directed at furthering the careers of their creators, or not damaging the promotion prospects of the marketing people, or are simply based on lazy thinking.

Ads are often forced to bend to many differing agendas; so they collect mandatories inclusions that aren't really about effective communication.

Like the standard 'liquid metal' beauty shot in car ads, the refreshed and delighted little shake of the drinker's head in beer ads, and the vacant, contented smile of mothers in practically all others ads.

The only mandatory on a creative brief should be "make it famous".

Steve Hadyn, one of the creative team behind Apple Computer's legendary '1984', is quoted as saying: "If you want to be a successful copywriter, write for the client; if you want to be an award winning copywriter, write for yourself; if you want to be an effective copywriter, write for the consumer."

Another thing that's come between the customer and a lot of great ideas is that advertising agencies make the mistake of styling themselves as a service industry. Far better the business should be considered a manufacturing business.

The product: Ideas.

Carefully assembled, tangible, muscular, artful and transforming ideas.

Admittedly, the manufacture process is somewhat elaborate and fraught at the moment. Finding a way to guarantee that the idea will overcome the process is the marketers' real challenge today.

A complicating aspect of this problem is that advertising agencies no longer seem to have the relationship with, or indeed command the respect of, senior company people. And without a champion at the highest level of the client company, a great idea deteriorates with each and every meeting. Layers of indecision breed abominable no-men.

(There's a legendary story from the halcyon days of British advertising in the 1970s, when things were quite different - the MD of the client company invited a particular agency principal, who was pitching for his account, to ask a few relevant questions of him regarding the business

The client MD had a bell on his desk, he explained, that he would ring in precisely 30 minutes, and the meeting would be over.

"How many layers of people have to approve the final campaign?" was the agency principal's first question.

"Seven," answered the client.

"Then ring the bell.")

What's all this got to do with The Law of Taste?

Well, as you'll see, "taste" is one example of the hollow virtues that clients so fondly and automatically mandate in their category. 'Taste' is frequently a piece of baggage that an idea is forced to carry in order to progress through the food chain toward the actual consumer.

Whether for good, lazy or political reasons, such category mandates are frequently misguided. As New York legend, and customer champion, Allen Rosenshine, explains.

THE LAW OF TASTE BY ALLEN ROSENSHINE

There is a long-standing phenomenon regarding "taste" in food and beverage advertising. And by that, I do not mean "taste" in the sense of style or tone or production values. I mean "taste" in the literal sense of the taste of the product as an advertised claim.

It is simply that "taste" as a consumer benefit in food and beverage advertising is an almost always used claim, but very infrequently is it a persuasive claim in establishing a competitive brand position. That is, motivating the consumer to select one brand over another.

If this is so, the more time and effort that goes into communicating good or great taste in advertising the brand, the more "taste makes waste."

Of course, as with any rule, there are exceptions. And we'll get to them. But first, let's examine the premise.

From the standpoint of the consumer, is taste a legitimate benefit? Certainly it is. I cannot imagine research on a food or beverage brand that would not prove conclusively that consumers give high priority to taste satisfaction as a brand attribute. Ask consumers what they want from a particular food or beverage and the consistent response is, not surprisingly, taste.

The real question is, if consumers keep telling us they want taste, does that mean they're not getting it?

I think there are very few if any food and/or beverage categories that are characterised by tasting bad. The reason consumers are always telling us in benefit/attribute or focus group research that they want "great taste" is because it's the natural focus of the eating and drinking experience.

So taste is the most important thing we want in our food and drink to the point that it is generic, and we should expect that research would consistently produce that conclusion.

Another reason we can bet on this is the fact that consumers are not usually creative in their answers to marketing and advertising research. They tend to play back essentially what the category's advertising has told them is important.

It is not that they can't think for themselves. Far from it, the consumer is very shrewd and discerning when it comes to deciding what they want or don't want to buy. (If they were dumb and easily manipulated, as many critics of advertising would have it, why do the vast majority of new products fail?). It is rather that consumers don't spontaneously play back their often impulsive and emotional reasons for brand selection. What they do tell us is the most obvious rational answer that comes to mind. And that turns out to be what they've seen in the advertising and experienced themselves. When it comes to food and beverages, the top-of-mind issue is taste.

One of the unfortunate results of food marketing research is that consumers say they want taste, so we advertise taste, so that they say they want taste. With this circular reasoning, it is not surprising that the history of food advertising is marked by so much that is indistinguishable, undifferentiating and therefore wasteful. Rather, we should concentrate on research that uncovers unfulfilled wants and needs — in other words, problems.

Ask the very same consumers who told us they wanted "great taste" in a food or beverage to respond to potential problems with that product and we will be surprised to learn that "it doesn't taste good" is very rarely, if ever, a high ranking problem. Rather, we may learn that "it takes too long to prepare" or "it's fattening" or "it can't be eaten on the run" or "it's too messy for kids" or a multitude of other considerations all of which are, in reality, bigger concerns, bigger wants and bigger problems than "taste."

A good example comes from research done some years ago in the category of canned dog food. (As "our best friends," I think they qualify for this discussion.) The results were that the purchasers (not the consumers, of course) wanted dog food that provided complete, well-balanced nutrition and a food the dog will like. Is it any wonder we've seen so much dog food advertising that basically says, "It's good for them and they'll love it"?

The same dog owners were concurrently asked to evaluate their problems with canned dog food. The highest-ranking complaints were that (1) it's too messy and (2) it smells awful.

In fact, all canned dog foods offer total balanced nutrition and dogs will eat every bit of just about any brand. But a lot of dry dog food get sold by solving the mess and smell problems. Yes, the purchaser was of course assured their dog would like the taste (which they probably assumed anyway) but that wasn't the point, or the point of difference of the advertising.

Even when we have a testable, provable statistical advantage in taste over competition, very rarely is that an effective strategy.

"Our chocolate pudding tastes better than their chocolate pudding" is of questionable motivating power because the consumer really doesn't think the chocolate pudding they're eating tastes bad to begin with. They wouldn't be eating it if it did, since the only reason, rational or otherwise, to eat chocolate pudding is because it tastes good. It's just not a problem.

You may get the sales force standing and cheering at a sales meeting with some we're-better-than-they-are advertising but the consumer is very likely unmoved by it.

I once asked our research department to review all the food and beverage advertising we had studied to establish any correlation between positive taste playback and the scores of the commercials in terms of memorability and/or motivation to purchase. The answer was no correlation.

A high positive taste playback did not mean a high memorability or persuasion score. In fact, it is quite understandable for advertising that does not impart anything new or interesting to be totally forgettable.

But while I advocate that we avoid the knee-jerk reaction of building food and beverage creative strategies that first and foremost demand communication of "great taste," I also want to suggest examples in which "taste" should be a major concern.

Despite the tremendous growth of health-oriented foods over the past couple of decades and given the well-publicised obesity problems in the US, there still seems to be a built-in resistance to the logic of eating what is good for you in favour of the pure emotional enjoyment of sugar, salt and fat.

In most categories, there is a "ceiling" effect that health-oriented foods and beverages come up against. What seems to happen is that the health segment of a category develops in response to advertised "breakthroughs" but eventually growth grinds to a halt regardless of media weight. In effect, we reach and persuade the psychologically attuned segment which is willing to trade off "taste" for "health"; but beyond that segment, there is little willingness to give up the pleasures of taste for the benefits of health.

It is a very complex psychology at work, because the health-oriented segment will expect a lower level of taste gratification and indeed will almost not trust the health claim if the product tastes too good. On the other hand, you can't grow the brand beyond the limitations of that segment unless you promise and deliver good taste.

An ongoing example of this is the diet cola category.

Advertising invariably delivers the constant assurance that the latest diet cola new product delivers taste as good as full-calorie colas. Even if blind taste tests show otherwise, most diet cola drinkers ultimately convince themselves of good taste in their diet colas to the point where they in fact no longer like the taste of the regular version.

I think this is because (1) they logically determined that they would drink the diet cola because of the weight control benefit and (2) they need to believe that the taste is just as good if not better than regular colas, so that they can get the satisfaction they want from their cola consumption.

An example of growth beyond the "ceiling" is Life Cereal, which was positioned when introduced as a high-protein, good-for-you brand. It had a foothold share but not a profitable business. Too much media money had to be spent to maintain that share against the "ceiling" effect of health versus taste.

In fact, contrary to the natural assumption for a healthy food, it actually tasted quite good. But it was not until a commercial showed a little kid named Mikey blessing Life Cereal's taste in spite of his brother's negativism about the cereal being good for them that Life Cereal sales took off and became the only cereal introduced in a span of two decades that was among the Top 10 in sales.

The critical insight in this case was that the advertising convinced mothers that their kids would like the taste and indeed they did. The actual consumers — the kids — were oblivious to the health claim and therefore the dynamic of the "ceiling" effect did not apply to them.

In the beer category, good taste is an assumed given unless, as with health claims for other food or beverages, something suggests that the taste might be compromised. More important is what I will call the "consumption milieu or mentality" that governs the beer - drinking experience to the point that a literal offering of fewer calories was impossible in establishing the "light beer" category.

Gablinger's, one of the first low-calorie beers, also promised real beer taste. But red-blooded beer drinkers, at the bar or the ballgame with their buddies or at home watching TV, don't want to be seen as worried about calories. And they naturally assumed that low-calorie beer had to have a watered-down taste. Gablinger's failed.

Lite Beer from Miller came at the lower-calorie content a whole new way. They didn't say "fewer calories" but rather "less filling" which meant that you could drink more of it. That was the real claim and the real news. Sure, they said "great taste" but they showed bar rooms full of America's most masculine popular heroes enjoying the beer exactly as they'd enjoy any beer, with the breakthrough benefit being that they could enjoy more of it.

The brilliant insight that launched Lite Beer was that it had nothing to do with the "great taste" they constantly proclaimed. It was all about being "less filling." And it established an entire category of beer that was not so much seen as better for your waistline but rather beer you could drink more of.

In all these cases, taste in the traditional sense would have been pure waste. In each case, taste was indeed an important issue but it had to be dealt with in a unique way based on insightful understanding of the role that taste actually played in positioning the brand's other characteristics.

But, you might be thinking, what about one of the most blatant taste superiority claims ever made in a category for which we've already observed that taste is practically generic? What about "The Pepsi Challenge" in which Pepsi blatantly advertised that it tastes better than Coke and showed consumer taste tests to prove it? Didn't that build Pepsi sales and in fact drive the Coca-Cola Company to introduce New Coke, positioned as tasting better?

In fact, the markets in which Pepsi sales improved significantly were markets in which they had only a very minor share of market compared to Coke, and in those markets, Coke sales actually grew as well. In other words, "The Pepsi Challenge" energised these markets, producing increased sales for both Pepsi and Coke by taking market share from the marginal brands.

It was good for Pepsi, of course, but not in the way you would have expected. And Coke's eventual reaction, the introduction of a better tasting New Coke, was the emotional result of seeing their brand attacked. Remember, they weren't losing share.

Worse yet, in responding, they unbelievably misunderstood the heritage and the role of taste in their own brand. People drink Coke because they like it but even more because they like what the brand stands for as an American icon.

That was, and still is, the competitive foundation for the Coke brand. It was not the taste, as Coke management learned when middle America greeted New Coke with all the enthusiasm of a newly discovered act in a Wagnerian opera. The ultimate irony of this cosmic marketing blunder is that the failure of New Coke bred a new appreciation for the existing product that was renamed and re-energised as Coke Classic.

While they averted disaster, taste nearly "wasted" one of the most successful brands in the history of marketing.

I'll add one more concern to the food and beverage advertising recipe. The problem again stems from the treatment of taste as a primary product claim. It is the way in which we test taste perceptions in our advertising.

I alluded earlier to the fact that there is often no correlation between taste playback in advertising and the memorability or motivation of that advertising. However, there is the very real possibility that this is a flaw in the testing systems, not a blanket condemnation of taste communication in food and beverage advertising.

The fact is, most of our frequently used testing systems measure only literal playback. They are not equipped to measure impressions or perceptions.

There are more advanced testing protocols that can indeed get closer to what advertising actually communicates non-literally and how it really works in affecting consumer attitudes and behaviour. However, most such systems are expensive and time consuming, and are therefore not attuned to most marketers' needs for positive sales and profit results every quarter of their fiscal years.

Because people are not equipped to verbalize their feelings very well and no non-verbal stimulus or response mechanism is usually supplied to recognise and evaluate emotions evoked by advertising, taste, which is not top-of-mind as a concern or problem, is not necessarily played back, even if it has been built into the advertising very prominently and literally.

On the other hand, it may be very much a part of the consumer's perception of the brand but when asked "what does the commercial or ad say or show," the answer is literally only what they remember, which is keyed only to whatever is responsive to their concerns and problems. Thus, even when taste is indeed an important part of the communication, as we have seen it can be, we are confounded by testing that does not properly measure its impact.

Perhaps the most memorable advertising for Burger King was a campaign created in the early to mid-70s called "Have it Your Way."

The commercials were replete with tasty, mouthwatering shots of sizzling meat, juicy tomatoes, crisp lettuce, onions, pickles, the works, but the differentiating competitive claim was a hamburger the way you want it, without the waiting.

Choice and speed were the consumer concerns so that addressing them produced motivating, effective advertising. (In the spirit of full disclosure, I must admit it was done by my agency, as was "The Pepsi Challenge," but that's ancient history.)

The taste playback in Burger King advertising might have been minimal, but that didn't mean we didn't communicate it. Now, if "great taste" had been a part of the strategy — for most food and beverages, it is — we could have fallen into the trap of downgrading the advertising because the research didn't play it back even though it was there. This happens all too often.

The strategy says taste, we build in literal taste claims in words and pictures, but it doesn't play back because it's not top-of-mind for the consumer, and it isn't the brand position we are advertising for people to remember and act on. Had decisions been made primarily on the communication of taste, a very successful marketing strategy would have gone to waste.

The conclusion is not to treat taste as the reason-for-being, when in fact it is an expected characteristic of the product, but rather to treat it as a reassurance and not expect to have research play it back on a literal basis.

Beer marketers have learned to do this as a way of life. After all, how can you communicate taste if you're not allowed to show the product being tasted (it is in fact illegal to show beer actually being drunk in commercials airing in the US)? You do it by creating a non-verbal, non-literal imagery that defines taste enjoyment and you don't make "great taste" the determining criterion in the research. After all is said and done, the big, leading beer brands are built on attitude, not product specifics. Recalling Lite Beer, the idea of "less filling" plays to the beer-drinking experience, not the caloric content.

So, am I suggesting that taste should not be a significant factor in food and beverage advertising? No. I am suggesting that there are valid and important reasons for taste claims but they are far fewer than our tendency to automatically assume that taste must be a primary part of communication.

What I am suggesting is that taste, when it is a strategic communication need — usually relegated to an assurance role subordinate to some other claim — should not be the concern it too often is. It ought only to be seen in the context of how the consumer sees it, which is often something taken for granted.

At the end of the day, advertising should (1) provide a positive, enjoyable, entertaining experience with the brand, or (2) communicate how the brand is particularly relevant to the prospect's lifestyle or way of thinking, or (3) offer something new for the category, or (4) all of the above.

Making "taste" the primary claim for most food and beverages will rarely meet any of these criteria and will usually result in the advertising being a waste.

THE LAW OF
TOPICALITY

P
lease write the introductory pages to the Law of Topicality yourself.

It's simple. Think of something interesting that happened today. Anything. Yes, that'll do. Now, isn't that far more magnetic to the wandering mind and excitable eye than reading a business book?

OK. That's an example of the Law of Topicality.

Real life, even at its most mundane, is usually more compelling than advertising.

Or even reading about advertising.

THE LAW OF TOPICALITY BY MICHAEL NEWMAN

How to talk persuasively about topical and tactical advertising in a book? A medium more about shelf life than it is about plugging into the zeitgeist of whatever exact moment you happen to be reading these words.

But I guess the issue of the day will always be, how to make truly lively advertising that stands in relief to the usual white noise, whether your today is May 2004 or May 4002.

Being topical isn't so easy when the advertising process itself is so killing to freshness and immediacy.

An average ad is worked over an average of 30 times in meetings from concept to despatch. No wonder so many end up so average.

Really, that any idea at all survives this proctology with integrity intact is remarkable. And in truth, only a handful of ads each year *do* manage to overcome the process and successfully go out into the real world and mix with the mainstream of life.

It's worth the effort. Successful Topical ads enjoy tremendous effectiveness compared to the spend behind them. So even though the things I'm going to talk about in this chapter will break a few comfortable systems, the ROI is AOK.

Nevertheless, let me start my saying that it's a tough ask. Hard for advertising ideas to compete with everyday news on the street; harder still, then, to be the news.

Nevertheless, that's precisely what I'm recommending your advertising strive to do. At least, occasionally.

Because, just as nothing's as stale as yesterday's news, there's most likely nothing is as fusty as your current advertising strategy.

Sorry, but it was, after all, based on yesterday's perspective. It's the age old, driving-with-the-rear-vision-mirror problem.

There's so much process, time and effort involved in the preliminaries to running most every advertising campaigns today, that nearly everyone else in your category has had the same period to digest, and react to, the marketing situation as you.

Meanwhile, they've read the same books, believed the same research, subscribed to the same journals and dealt with the same ever-shrinking choice of globalized, systematized agency networks.

On the other hand, nothing's as powerful for a brand as an immediate, vivacious, topical idea that captures a collective moment and blossoms around the water coolers and coffee tables of the world.

Passing the 'water cooler test' (by now this is probably becoming the 'SMS test' in many young markets around the globe) should be mandatory on every brief.

Aim for fame.

"You can't underestimate the water cooler factor" said Pepsi's Dave DeCecco in the New York Times, in February 2004, when talking about the power of big events, "…. to unveil new advertising."

There's no time like The Present.

Because, that's what your customer is talking about; and thinking about; and coping with: The Present. If your campaign is good enough, it might become part of this constant flux of present-tense consciousness and, hopefully, even enter the vernacular.

If your starting point is what is actually happening today and, more importantly, if your advertising department has the necessary speed to market, then your brand will be in a world of your own.

A class of one. Out in the clear. On people's lips. On the button. Of the 'now'.

Usually such ads are one-offs; a brilliant comment on the times that sparkles and resonates with the moment, and combines it with the brand's intent.

"Better a wild, wonderful, one-off idea that seizes a moment and makes a whole country laugh," says former Saatchi & Saatchi creative director, Kim Thorp.

He means better to have something savvy and scrappy than a tired and solid campaign that has the stakeholders all nodding their heads; while the consumers are nodding off.

Whilst Consistency is a Law, Predictability can be a Crime.

Great topical ads take a 'newsworthy' snippet of popular culture, and use it as proof of the brand's campaign, or promise, or claim.

This may sound more like jazz improvisation than careful campaign orchestration, but providing that good strategies are in place as a platform, this is a more spirited approach than rigidly sticking to well-worn patterns. The sheer energy of an occasional Topical ad breathes life into a brand.

This is because people are more interested in the attitudes of a brand than its features these days. Features are table stakes. Show us where your heart lies.

We want the ground truth.

The world over, in every category, we're talking to an increasingly ad literate and media savvy consumer. So a solid, plodding reinterpretation of last year's execution isn't always the most pungent way to build brand equity.

Yes, it is about planning spontaneity. Unfortunately, few organizations respond fast enough to take advantage of moments of shared culture. There are exceptions, of course. A few have built their brand's fortunes on an authentic dialogue with the world, conducted through media advertising.

Bennetton was one; Branson's Virgin another, I guess. They outmanoeuvred the big, slow guys; and that's why every regional and domestic market has an example or two to talk about.

In the Beginning was Word of Mouth

From international events to suburban book launches, from global sports involving millions of people right down to your friend's friend's flat-warming, 'partied communication' is integral to our lives.

Humans, more than any animal, have invented events and social gatherings – rocks concerts, religious celebrations, birthday parties, engagements, weddings, seminars, football matches, rallies, graduations, hen parties, buck's nights and the rest; it is all about shared experience. Social circuit breakers; opportunities to flaunt status, to pool knowledge and opinion.

Shared experience is one of the essential values we enjoy about relationships with friends, relatives and marriage partners for generations.

Physically, when we Homo sapiens finally emerged to stand on our hind legs, and the shape of our evolving jaw and oral cavity began providing the capacity for speech, it was about the same time (give or take a few hours), that communal food began to be stored. In short, such advances meant the mouth now had time and opportunity to do other things.

And that's when 'word of mouth' advertising was invented.

(According to the Danish linguist, Otto Jesperson, there are five theories on the origin of language. The Bow-wow Theory, that speech arose through people copying the sounds of their environment. The Pooh-pooh Theory, that people started emitting instinctive sounds caused by emotions like pain, anger, frustration or similar. The Ding-dong Theory, that people reacted to external stimuli to produce sounds that were harmonious with the environment – arguably 'mama' is the sound made when the lips approach the breast. Then there's the Yo-yo Theory, that argues speech arose as a collaborative effort as people worked together communally, their physical effort producing rhythmic grunts that became in time, chants and eventually language. The La-la Theory suggests the romantic side of life was the primary agency for the development of language. The love, play, feeling, need for song, soaring emotion and poetry.

You won't be surprised that, in 1866, the Linguistic Society of Paris resolved that, because of the noisy, vehement and disorderly meetings, any further formal discussion of the origin of language was to be banned.)

Word of mouth has been making people feel more comfortable with their environment for about 100,000 years – nowadays, by talking about and recommending brands.

According to The Anatomy of Buzz by US marketer Emanuel

Rosen, "Recent surveys show that 58% of young people rely to some extent on others when selecting a car, 53% of moviegoers follow the recommendations of friends and 65% of the people who bought a palm organizer were inspired by the enthusiasm of others."

Everyone knows word of mouth adds fame and currency to the brand when ordinary people say, "Did you see that ad last night where...?"

The new cleaner in my city apartment was quite interested when he heard that I was a partner in an advertising agency. "Really," he said, as he swept the floor, "I know all about advertising."

"Really?" I responded, thinking of the many clients who'd also said that.

"Yeah," said the cleaner, "it's all about getting people to talk about your product."

He was right, I said immediately. (Then I thought how many marketers should be sweeping floors.) And there it was in a nutshell: The Law of Topicality.

Just as "new" is the most powerful word in advertising, so 'news' is the ultimate aim of advertising. Because if you're newsworthy, you've got the most powerful advertising technique in the world working for your brand.

Look at it like this. What do people talk about? The weather. What they have to do later in the day. What somebody said about what they've been doing. Current things. Contemporary, ordinary things. Things that texture the ebb and flow of the times. Flotsam and jetsam.

'The now', in short. So, as Shakespeare's Edgar said to Gloucestor, "Ripeness is all. Come on!"

In the Middle was the Process

A certain pretentiousness, it's been noted, overtakes marketing people when writing about their product.

Perhaps this jargonised frame of reference has somehow led to advertising's own clichéd language, and its limited set of category-imagery.

Advertising is using fewer and fewer words and images, of less and less variety. To worse and worse effect.

We arrange words and images about so-called real aspects of people's lives, and shallowly and cheese-ily tangle and abuse them. The same old thing regurgitated with less imagination than last time.

We take the lively soil of real life and sanitize it until it is heavy as a clod.[1] Yet as Samuel Johnson wrote, "words are the daughters of the earth."

Too many advertisements lack dexterity and lifeblood. They lack a wide enough brand vocabulary to do any thing other.

Most brands attempts at tapping into popular culture are as insightful as turning a baseball cap around backwards and thinking that's cool. Heavy handed, method acting. Undemanding, hollow, with all eccentricity and quirky liveliness eradicated. Originality as anathema.

This contributes to the wall of advertising sameness, and the audience sees only the usual comfortable, expected patterns. So it notices little.

Similarities merge into formula. Like in Hollywood. (As someone once asked: "Those "Rocky" movies, how can you tell them apart?"

The answer came: "It's easy; they're numbered").

Ironically, consumer choice and worldliness has expanded in inverse proportion, as the marketing vocabulary has shrunk.

And it's getting worse, with a breed of myopic brand-nazis now rising, who are rigidly keeping new life from campaigns in the guise of being so called 'brand guardians'. Both agencies and clients have them. They exert relentless daily pressure over every nervous aspect of their charge. Yet, there's no prize for mere uniformity. A mere C.I. (Corporate Identity) is not a strategy or an idea.

Brands die of stasis.

Legal departments also deserve a heavy sentence here. With more lawyers than art directors involved in advertising, many companies are askance at the notion of actually being in the news. That usually means having to deny something bad that's happened. No, no…, you see we try and avoid publicity.

(As one Compliance Advisor recently said to me: "Of course, we don't expect our marketers to be lawyers."

"Why then," I couldn't help asking, "do you let your lawyers to be marketers?")

Legal fees are now very significant items in marketing budgets, and so many want to be seen as having their existence justified.

So, for one reason or another, many wheels are spun but little forward progress is made.

---

[1] It's ironic, as Don Watson's book, *Death Sentence – The Decay of Public Language* points out, that at the same time, the English language is growing at the rate of 20,000 words a year. (There's a term for this; neologism, or neology: a recently coined word or phrase, or a recently extended meaning of an existing word or phrase.)
Plus, for every new word, several old ones gain added new means each year.

Brand language should be creative and rigorous. Not sullenly predictable and impoverished of spirit.

After the CBS broadcast from Superbowl XXXV111 in 2004 (in many ways, a spiritual home for the wonderful one-off topical ad since Apple's '1984'), there were complaints that ads for Bud Light, Charmin, Cialis, Lay's, Levitra, Sierra Mist were almost as tasteless as the antics of the performers, Janet Jackson, Justin Timberlake and Nelly, in the halftime show.

This uproar led to calls that the big event TV programs, like the Grammy Awards and future Super Bowls, be more controlled.

Interestingly, the ABC network, which broadcasts the Academy Awards in the US, already had a system in place to scrutinize every TV commercial scheduled to run during the show. Commercials have to undergo two separate screenings for ABC, from script stage and storyboards right through to finished 'tapes'.

This is Spontaneity Hell. And it may be your future.

In the End, You're Either Famous or Just Making up the Numbers

William Goldman, the illustrious US film maker, once commented on those trying to analyse the success of his Butch Cassidy and the Sundance Kid: "They tried all kinds of ways to analyse why it was so successful; but I'll tell you why. The only reason some movies are successful is that people like them. If they're not successful, it's because people didn't like them. The rest is pathology."

Of course, famous can also be infamous. All is equal under The Law of Topicality.

The Church of England in Birmingham recently ran a campaign with poster headlines like: "Body piercing? Jesus had his done 2,000 years ago."

Blasphemous? Probably. But the Anglican High Church answered criticism by saying: "Anything which makes an impact on the secular society is of value."

American actress, Demi Moore, had just done her striking Vanity Fair cover while heavily pregnant, but that didn't stop this Toyota Camry ad becoming the most complained about print advertisement in Australian history, at the time.

And it only ran once.

Nevertheless, the new concept of a "wide-body car" was successfully introduced, both economically and quickly, before a cent of the main campaign budget had been spent.

Everyone involved on an advertising account — the creatives, suits, and clients — should scour every newspaper, every morning, with a mind to finding some buried ammunition that might be turned into a topical or tactical ad.

Of course, topical ads can be used quite aggressively. For example, we once bought an outdoor poster site for Toyota that was positioned opposite the entrance to the Ford factory, and could be seen by every one of their executives as they drove into work each morning. Deliciously competitive tactics.

You can contrive the moment, as with the Cannes winning "Bugger" commercial for Toyota Hilux: to avoid over-exposing the famously popular ad, the agency took the TVC off air; then spiked interest in it again and again with a series of topical and tactical reminders in other media.

For example, after the huge fireworks on the spans of the Sydney Harbour Bridge at midnight on New Year's Eve, we ran a full-page ad the following morning showing a retouched shot of the bridge in cinders, and the caption: "Bugger."

That's an example of a topical ad you might be able to plan for. It's not hard. Every Valentines Day, my local florist has a chalk sign that promises: "Flowers today, fireworks tonight".

The richness of eventful life should be celebrated by advertising brands.

Other examples, like for Landcruiser, sometimes fall into your lap.

The brand's indestructible image was far from dented when a Landcruiser was destroyed by the Australian Air Force. They accidentally dropped an unarmed bomb on it. The photo was on the front page of every newspaper.

Next day, we ran a topical ad admitting that, yes, perhaps there is one way to destroy a Landcruiser.

In 2004, a campaign for coffee in Australia, by M&C Saatchi, was launched using hotly debated social issues, like the refugee question, as the platform.

In December 2003, a brand new advertising agency network called DNA opened its doors.

Happily for everyone, quite soon after this, Iraq's Saddam Hussein was found and identified ... by his DNA. You may have seen it on the news?

Anyway, two days later, this ad was on page 5 of the newspaper and suddenly everyone was talking more about the new agency than the old dictator.[2]

Big problems are solved by DNA

DNA - Agency Network, call Michael Newman or John Poulakakis on (03) 9645 9710

---

[2] One of this book's contributors, James Lowther, author of the chapter The Law of Humour, congratulated me on DNA's Saddam ads. "Great to see [your new agency] already has a world class Dictator working for it."

*

Topical p.s. – In today's newspaper (my today, not yours) is an interview with Sun Microsystems vice president of global communications and marketing, Andy Lark, who suggests advertisers and their agents have for too long toiled at making marketing buttoned up and perfect.

He asserts that fear of failure clogs the system like cholesterol filled artery that ultimately and drastically reduces the company's performance. He advises us to develop a 'kill it fast' mentality. "We grew up in a culture of let's get the brochure perfect, the ad has to be perfect – that you can't fail as a marketer.

"It needs to change to fail it fast."

This theory might sound drastic, but who can argue that Campaigns need to deliver quickly these days? Attention spans are shrinking, magazine readership is falling and TV viewing is fading.

Maybe the future is not about sustained, low level activity. But something far fresher and energetic.

You tell me. After all, you're already there.

THE LAW OF THE SILVER ELEPHANT

This is a *great* chapter. Because there's too much *good* in the world. Too many good, solid campaigns. Too many good, sound people. Too many good meetings. Too few great successes.

Can a good idea become a great idea? How do you recognise great creative people?

The bad news first: A good idea, with more research and analysis, more time and a bigger budget, will not transform into great. Great comes from a different set of values altogether. It's no point sharpening the same pencil.

As New Zealand ad guru Kim Thorpe once observed: "Good doesn't deliver the slap on the back at cocktail parties or a desk piled with letters of praise from customers, or the TV interviews, or the follow up stories in the women's magazines. Good doesn't stir up much emotion at all."

How do great creative people have great ideas?

When Sir Charlie Chaplin was asked how he got his ideas, he explained: "Ideas come from an intense desire for them; continually desiring, the mind becomes a watch-tower on the look-out for incidents that may excite the imagination … elimination from accumulation is the process … sheer perseverance to the point of madness. One must have a capacity to suffer anguish and sustain enthusiasm over a long period of time. Perhaps it's easier for others, but I doubt it."

A more recent humorist, Douglas Adams, agreed; he suggested writing creatively was a straightforward matter of "staring at a piece of paper until your ears bleed."

Great creative people are driven to extremes, looking for notions from the periphery of thinking. And, not surprisingly, a great idea is often harder to sell to clients than a more familiar notion, more difficult to produce, puts more strain on the client-agency relationship and sometimes involves working with difficult people.

Nevertheless, to be successful, a brand must allow a great idea into its bosom and confront its key business issue. A transformation of that issue should be the simple objective. This means setting a challenge that is big, bold, ambitious – the greatest imaginable.

If you will it, it is no longer a dream.

Aim to set the standard. High enough for your competition to envy.

Too many campaigns are written to maintain the status quo. That's why they're average.

Advertising used to aim for memorability, but that's setting your sights way too low. Shoot for fame. Great will get people talking. Word of mouth spreads a brand more persuasively than any media budget.

People talk about great ads and they become fans of brands.

Fame means you're always in the consideration set. Famous brand lines and icons become part of the popular culture lexicon.

Great advertising keeps the brand continually fresh and allows it to pop into real-life conversations more naturally and, therefore, it makes recommendations easier.

Great ads deliver product placement in real life.

Ideas like these literally add a value to products over and above their actual product performance, the communication itself creating tangible value. There's a sense of belonging to something special.

Great ideas sink deep into the soil of memory and builds up an untapped cash reservoir of brand equity. A Japanese client of mine used to call it "the invisible benefit."

What's all this got to do with Silver Elephants? Founder of South Africa's famous agency, The Jupiter Drawing Room, Graham Warsop, believes you don't find what you're not looking for.

If you're hunting for great, big ideas, then you need some high-powered ammunition.

THE LAW OF THE SILVER ELEPHANT BY GRAHAM WARSOP

Introduction

At a glance, the various chapter headings in this book will leave most experienced practitioners of advertising nodding sagely. The Law of Simplicity, the Law of Relevance, the Law of Positioning ... there can be no denying the veracity of such irrefutable laws.

But can the same be said of a law that carries the cryptic title "The Law of the Silver Elephant"?

I hope so.

I hope to prove that one of the essential components of great advertising has less to do with executional theory and technique and everything to do with a particular state of mind. A state of mind that is so fundamental to the origination of outstanding advertising that it deserves to be enshrined in a law.

A Couple of Assumptions

This book is not concerned with laws that relate to the creation of advertising per se. No doubt, every law expounded could be ignored and something resembling advertising produced. What we're concerned with here is the irrefutable laws that govern the origination of *great* advertising, and by *great* advertising, I mean advertising that is sufficiently distinctive, compelling and relevant, that it stands out from its rivals in the category and results in increased sales and/or greater brand value for the product or service being advertised.

Also, one must not assume this particular law is limited to the predictable format of the 30-second television ad. This law embraces advertising in all its forms and guises. The dictionary defines *advertising* as meaning "to turn the mind or attention to" (from the Latin *ad* — to: *vertere* — to turn). Accordingly, for this law, the definition of advertising includes above the line, below the line, design and packaging. (Isn't packaging or packaging design there to turn the mind or attention to the brand?).

Defining the Law of the Silver Elephant

The Law of the Silver Elephant can be defined thus: *Great advertising (powerful, distinctive, relevant work that increases sales and builds brand value) relies on the imagination of one or more individuals who have the desire: (1) to bring something into the world that never existed before (2) to do so in such a way that it surpasses what has been done before.*

In England the law of murder requires two things to be proved. A mental intent (*mens rea*) and a physical act (*actus reas*). The Law of the Silver Elephant similarly has two components: the mental intent to produce something that has never been done before, and the physical act of successfully carrying out that intent.

Let's illustrate the Law of the Silver Elephant by way of an example. Two creative teams get exactly the same brief landing on their desk. The brief is a good one. Each team approaches it with a different mind-set.

Team One (The Path of Least Resistance Team)

"We've got this brief, we think we know what the client wants. They want something safe. And safe is probably right for this brand. They're going to research it so it'll help if the solution we propose has a familiarity about it — we know people gravitate towards advertising that has something familiar about it. Yup. That's the way to go on this one."

Team Two (The Silver Elephant Team)

"What can we do that'll make the solutions we propose really distinctive? Let's look at the work that's being done in the market for our client's competitors. We should be aiming to produce something that's never been done before in this category. It probably won't be an easy sell to the client, but if it's distinctive and stands out, if it's relevant and on brief, hopefully the client will see that it'll make his advertising spend work harder. We suspect that the client's looking for something safe but hopefully he'll realise that safe advertising is the riskiest advertising of all because it runs the risk of not being seen."

Let's make some more observations on our Silver Elephant team's mindset.

They are likely to share a common (or not so common) character trait. They are probably working for something more than money. They're governed by a desire to rise above the "me too" advertising formulas and create something truly original and distinctive. It may be that, in the great scheme of things, advertising is, as Neil French rightly observes, "not the most important thing in the world, not even one of the top million most important things in the world." But to them it is. To them, the smile on a face, the length of a dissolve, the choice of a particular typeface and its point size are worthy of much painstaking deliberation. Willingly sacrificing evenings and weekends to sit in an edit suite crafting, honing and refining the communication — it's not just about the money. There is a greater driving force and it's central to the success of most of the best work and most of the great advertising that is produced in the world. There is a personal satisfaction that comes from the act of creation, of bringing something into the world that never existed before and doing it in such a way that it will touch, delight, charm, persuade and seduce an audience.

Our Silver Elephant team will recognise that great advertising results when the driving force to create meets the rational need to sell. Where these paths converge, is where the greatness lies. It is in this soil that one will sow the seeds that reap such giant rewards for brands. If one looks at the example of luminaries such as Bernbach,

Ogilvy, Abbot, Hegarty and Delaney, you will note that they genuinely care about the success or failure of the brands they communicate. They are concerned with powerful advertising that is the servant, not the master, of a brand promise or positioning.

Our team's desire to create something better, something original lies at the very heart of this law. They ask themselves, why is the world so full of charmless ads? So many strategies translated into communications that lack flair? Everyone can mark a box that says strategically sound and safe. Few seem to go the extra mile and ask how does it make you feel? Few rise above the rational, appeal to the emotions and capture the imagination. Our team doesn't sit down to write an ad that's the 20th best, the 10th best or even the second best ad in a category. They aim to create the best they are capable of.

When you think about it, isn't the basis of all international advertising awards shows to recognise and reward work that has been brought into the world that didn't exist before, work that has been executed in such a way that it is better than anything else produced in that category in a given year?

Let's leave our creative team to soldier on with the brief.

The Law of the Silver Elephant really comes into its own as a driving force for great advertising, when the client/marketer/manufacturer exhibits the same desire to bring into the world something that has never existed before, to make it stand out from what has come before and to succeed in translating that desire into reality. Such clients believe in innovation. Supremely conscious of the "sea of sameness" that exists in most product categories today, they place enormous emphasis on the need to try to create a product or brand that genuinely stands out. They don't just rely on an advertising message to give distinction to their brand. They are likely to ask themselves the question (often), how can I make my car, shoes, confectionary (insert product here) original and extraordinary.

It is therefore fitting that the person chosen to embody the Law of the Silver Elephant was an inventor. A manufacturer. A brand owner. A client.

He was an Italian gentleman who represents the virtues of imagination, perseverance and vision (all Silver Elephant qualities) in such great measure. He made cars. And the cars he made took his name. Bugatti. A name that to this day stirs the heart of every lover of the great marques. Etorre Bugatti was born in 1881. At the age of 17 he left art school to pursue his passion for engineering. By the age of 29 he had opened his own factory and set about building some of the world's great automobiles. By the age of 40 he had achieved much. His Type 35 was acknowledged to be one of the greatest racing designs of its day. But that wasn't enough for Etorre. He decided he would undertake the design and production of the greatest motorcar the world had ever seen.

And so was born Etorre Bugatti's dream for the Royale, a car that would out do every single automobile that had come before it. Having conceived of the idea of bringing into the world something that had never existed before (*mens rea*) he set about turning that dream into reality (*actus reas*).

One cannot help but admire the grandeur of his vision and the determination he brought to his task. When the most expensive Rolls Royce of the day cost US$40 000, the Bugatti Royale would cost double that, just for the chassis. The car had a massive 14.7 litre engine – so powerful that second gear would take the car from virtually zero to 93mph. The design of the car was sublimely elegant despite its colossal size. (The overall length was more than 21 feet and the wheelbase was as long as two current Chevrolet Corvettes!) Very importantly, for Bugatti, building the biggest and most expensive car was not enough. It also had to be the best. Quality was everything.

In a world where marketers and their agencies increasingly use all the powers at their disposal to seduce, encourage, persuade and sometimes bamboozle prospective clients to buy, Etorre took precisely the opposite approach. So precious were his Royales, conceptually and actually, he wanted to not simply sell them, but to only sell them to owners who would truly appreciate them. Thus, prospective purchasers would need to apply to Mr Bugatti (or *Le Patron* as he was affectionately known) expressing their interest in the Royale. Receipt of an invitation to his home at Molsheim, Alsace (where the factory was situated) indicated the applicant had cleared the first hurdle. During the course of a weekend, Mr Bugatti would appraise potential purchasers to ensure they would do the Royale's name and reputation justice. Apparently his undisclosed criteria were said to include the conversational ability and even the table manners of the applicant.

It was a condition precedent of the weekend's evaluation that the applicant would be notified in writing of *Le Patron's* decision and no further correspondence would be entered into.

Imagine being briefed on the advertising campaign for a car that money alone could not buy.

It should come as no surprise that when deciding on the radiator mascot for the car, Etorre Bugatti did not conduct any focus groups. He did not evaluate Rolls Royce's Spirit of Ecstasy and seek to produce something to rival its celestial grace. He simply chose a sculpture created by his younger brother, Rembrandt Bugatti. It was of a standing, playing elephant. And so the elephant (not necessarily the most obvious or even the most appropriate symbol for a sublimely elegant car capable of achieving speeds of more than 125mph) took its place in history. The mascot was signed by the Valsuami Foundry (the most highly regarded foundry of its day) and cast in cire perdue silver.

Today it seems so many decisions are put in the hands of consumers. Rarely do marketers make a move without insisting a focus group wade through an animatic. God forbid, focus groups are even held to decide on the most popular endings for movies. The Law of the Silver Elephant challenges marketers to take the initiative to be bold, brave and confident enough to make their own decisions about what is right for their brands. To recognise that a "boring, staid, me-too, follow the leader, try and emulate the best competitor" mindset is the wrong one in these difficult and demanding times.

Sure, there will be those that point out that due to the Wall Street Crash, only six Bugatti Royale's were ever built, and of those, only three were ever sold new. To them, it might be worth pointing out that on a cold November evening in 1987, at London's Albert Hall, Christies sold a Bugatti Royale at auction for the price of £5 million, the world record price paid for an automobile.

There are, of course, bound to be plenty of people who will miss the entire point of the Law of the Silver Elephant. They will say that it's not always about building the biggest and the best. It will escape their attention that it is Etorre Bugatti's philosophy that is enshrined in the Law of the Silver Elephant — not literally his choice of vehicle (excuse the pun). He could have been the manufacturer of a bicycle, a washing machine or soap powder. The law has actually nothing to do with cars. Etorre is demonstrative of a state of mind, an attitude. It's about wanting to do something extraordinary and having the vision, perseverance, talent and imagination to succeed in accomplishing that endeavour.

It just so happened that Etorre Bugatti set out to build the biggest most expensive car the world had ever seen. Presumably the inventors of DaimlerChrysler's Smart car set out with pretty much the opposite objective, yet they honour the Law of the Silver Elephant every bit as much as Ettore Bugatti. The Smart car is an original. It stands out from everything else in the category. It embodies outstanding design and required vision and imagination to bring it into existence. (And maybe that's a point too. With genuine product differentiators, based on quality, becoming fewer and fewer, the importance of design is becoming greater and greater.)

Conclusion

It's important to recognise that everyday around the world, thousands of agencies produce solid workmanlike communications that probably do a reasonable job in the marketplace. But this chapter and this book are not concerned with advertising that does a reasonable job in the marketplace. It's concerned with work that through its originality and relevance does an outstanding job in the marketplace.

Etorre Bugatti was a visionary. He didn't run research groups to see what the gap in the market was. He didn't look at successful competitors and try and emulate them. He simply set out to create something from nothing. He set out to create something extraordinary.

The Law of the Silver Elephant is, it is suggested, a vital component in the quest for great advertising. At its best, it relies on the desire of both agency and client to want to bring into the world something that never existed before and to do it in such a way that it surpasses everything that has come before it. Both parties recognise that in a crowded cluttered marketplace, one word will conquer: imagination. Not just the imagination to conceive bold powerful ideas, but the imagination to bring new products, styles and designs to market. Both parties want to make the budget work harder by demanding, approving and rejoicing in work that breaks the code of the category. From an advertising stand point, the ability to translate that desire into actuality is an enormously valuable attribute. Clients should recognise this spark when they see it and should do everything in their power to kindle and not extinguish it. They should seek it out. Harness it. Reward it. They should know that it's important enough to be enshrined in a law and cast in stone. Or better still, in cire perdue silver.

THE LAW OF THE CHAT

"Who are we talking to?" is a question asked in the formulation of literally every ad campaign under the sun. The emphasis is always on the first word. It's about targeting.

However, the offence is forgetting about the second bit. The bit about *talking* to.

Traditionally, of course, advertising has "talked at." That's supposedly changed in recent years. But today's marketing jargon about conducting a dialogue with the consumer is mostly just that. Jargon.

Many marketers are trying to personalise their brands, pretending to be like real people and yet not quite making it. It's like faking sincerity. Glib. Unless you're real, and real careful, you end up with depersonalised personalisation.

Talking to a demographic is actually not the same as addressing one person directly. (It's the marketing equivalent of "I hear you" rather than "I am listening to you".)

What's required is a fundamental change. It has been described as a shift in emphasis from the era of "experts," to the era of the *storyteller*.

In communication terms, the human mind has evolved to absorb stories. Our genes have evolved specialised language modules in our brains, and stories inform our shared cultural memory.

If you know *who* it is that you want to empathise with your brand, then refocus away from telling them what to do and instead focus on what *they* really need and want.

And what people really want from your brand's advertising is engagement. They want dreams, memories, passion, and laughter. They want nourishing stories.

Not sales spiels.

Not speeches.

Not lectures.

Not product briefings.

Get used to the idea that no one is interested in learning about product features through advertising, anymore.

There are too many peddlers these days, a wise client once said to me, too many marketers have forgotten their roles. Marketers should be telling stories. Selling intangibles. That's how life insurance is sold, with stories — otherwise you're just offering a bit of coloured paper and a cheque when you die.

"Listen as I tell my tale with shameless sincerity," is how the master Italian filmmaker, Federico Fellini, defined the role. He said: "Our duty as storytellers is to walk people to the station ..." Do this appealingly, and they'll board your train.

Neil French, creative director of O&M Worldwide, and pioneer of high creativity for the Asian world, knows a thing or two about shameless sincerity. What follows is an enlightening fireside chat about how to *talk to* people once you decide "who you're talking to."

THE LAW OF THE CHAT BY NEIL FRENCH

When Mike asked me to do this piece, I came over all peculiar. The very idea of writing a whole chapter gave me the willies.

"But you're a copywriter," he said.

"That's exactly the point," I stammered. "I write little blobs of copy; little succinct arguments. Not sermons and soliloquies."

"Well, do your best," he said.

So I said I would.

Then I had *another* attack of the wobblies.

The book was to be called *Laws of Advertising and when to break them*. My view of all "laws," concerning any creative process (even one as marginally creative as doing ads), is that they should be broken on sight. This would mean that I would be proposing something that by its nature should be ignored.

There's a splendidly nihilistic philosophical point in there somewhere, but not one that justifies typing this out instead of sitting in the sun. I'd have leapt at the chance to do a chapter on "Outlaws" … but M.T., being younger and a lot more agile than I, grabbed it first. When this compendium is published, hers will be the first bit I'd read.

But then I got to thinking: Why *can't* I write lots? Why would I find it impossible to write a book? And I think I've cracked the answer.

To me, writing an ad is talking on paper. It's not really writing at all. It's just chat. And I know that given a juicy subject, I can hold an audience with an anecdote for just so long — and not a second longer. (Sadly, this skill softens, like so many things, with drink. Which is why you'll occasionally see me chatting merrily, early in the wee hours, to a dribbling drunk and the nice policeman who's trying to get me vertical.)

The Art of the Chat. There's a title for the book I'll never write. (And since this chapter has to do with "Laws" apparently, please feel free to substitute "Law" for "Art", and then, as recommended earlier, totally to ignore the fact that you've done so.)

There are no laws: the *art* is all about knowing your audience. The comatose drunk is not actually an audience since, to him, my glittering oratory is as the buzzing of a hive of wasps. The nice cop is not an audience as he's just glad I'm not blowing a feather-on-a-curly-thing at him, or singing "My Way." The audience was the group that seemed spellbound, half a bottle ago, and whom I've lost somewhere along the way.

Where did they go? And why?

Well, "where" is easy. "Anywhere out of earshot of this pillock" about covers it.

But why? I think, again, I know.

I lost them the moment I stopped talking one-on-one, and started pontificating to "the audience."

It's why most political speeches, and most sermons, are so bloody boring. The speaker has a message for everyone, and insists on *speaking* to everyone. Whereas the trick is to talk to one person in a room, in the knowledge that many others will also think you're speaking only to them, personally and intimately.

It is widely acknowledged that when Adolf Hitler ranted at the massive Nuremberg rallies, every member of his audience felt he, personally, was being asked to come to the aid of the Fuhrer.

When Churchill spoke on the radio of "fighting on the beaches", millions of men and women saw themselves as standing next to Winston on the shingle, staring defiantly out to sea.

Jack Kennedy was talking to the young, the idealistic, the generation that saw him as a younger, sexier version of Dad, when he exhorted them to ask, "What you can do for your country." You — singular.

And that's how great ads work. When you read them you feel that this was aimed directly at you. In your heart you know that thousands like you are feeling the same, but that doesn't spoil it. In a way, it enhances it: you're a member of a select club.

When you see a long-copy ad, you know that it's aimed at you, because you're an avid reader. So you read it — until, like the slurring old sod, it bores you. When you see a witty visual joke, you feel closer to the brand — largely because you know that so many people won't "get it." That's how Yoof-marketing works. And one day, when it dawns on the brand-owners that the grey-dollar is more numerous and more cynical than any other, that's how they'll have to talk to the geezers.

The splendid and indispensable thing that we all have at our disposal, as writers and producers of advertising, is a choice of medium.

Let me lumber you with another of my hobbyhorses: I think all advertising is, to some extent, crass and rude. Let us count the ways:

The bumph that clogs up your letterbox every day. An irritating pile of paper and a waste of perfectly good trees. You have to shuffle through it all to get at the bills and the letter from Auntie Maisie. And most irritating of all are the pieces *disguised* as bills or letters from Auntie M.

"Spam" in your email. We won't even deign to discuss.

Television ads. Imagine for a moment that you and your family are watching … I don't know … Formula One racing, for instance. Just as Eddie Irvine has stuffed his Jag into the old tires again, and Shuey is about to carve bits off Coulthard, into your living-room leaps a man in a suit who stands in front of the screen and tries to sell you a car! And he's there legally, and he won't go away! That is what we do for a living. (Personally, I will never, *ever* buy a Honda-*anything*, as long as I live, on account of their ill-placed, ill-timed, patronising Formula One ads. But that's the point. People take our rudeness *personally*.)

Radio, I suppose, is less rude, as nobody actively *listens* to radio anyway; and, in any case, the ads are generally *so* bad they're impossible to take any note of at all. If you're one of the perpetrators of radio ads, please note that a funny voice is not an idea, and a funny voice shouting is even less of one. Try saying something interesting. But then, you probably don't *know* anything interesting. (See? You can insult a radio-ad writer so easily, in the same way that they take such pains to insult your own intelligence. They won't notice you, any more than you'd notice them.)

Print Media. Magazines, for instance. I've never actually been *annoyed* by magazine ads, except for the mass of them at the beginning of GQ. They're annoying merely because they're all the same, can't possibly work, and account for half of the weight of the mag. Nevertheless, they're not what I bought the thing for, and thus they're rude for being there at all. On the other hand, they pay most of the cost of the mag, so I'll put up with them.

Newspapers. Now, I have to admit to being a huge fan of newspapers. With the exception of some appallingly vast tomes in the US, there's never enough advertising to be an annoyance. And the *best* newspaper ads are witty and current, and occasionally intelligent. Again, I think I'm intelligent, and I'm flattered if someone addresses me as such.

So there it is. Advertising that appears to be talking solely to one individual is a lot less rude than the "Ere, you lot! Listen to this!" school of communication.

Now, let's go into that in some depth.

Hello.

Hello!

Why are you dribbling on my table? And who is this nice man in blue?

THE LAW OF NICE

C ut throat, dog eat dog, every man for himself, attack is the best defence ... you know what I mean, it's a jungle out there and everyone is trying to bite your back. Yet much of this book preaches likeability, warmth, emotion and humanity.

So let's be frank, it's hard to be genuinely warm in a cold-hearted business. Nevertheless, advertising is the business of ideas, it's imagination applied to marketing, it's an instinctual evolutionary tool developed as a means of ensuring survival in this jungle.

Which means the somewhat rational process of getting to a great ad must be carefully constructed so as to avoid throwing gems onto the slagheap.

The idea must be allowed to overcome the procedure. Otherwise, the machinations can be tough-minded, sleekly efficient and produce a campaign that pleases all the brand stakeholders, and will unfortunately still fail miserably in the real world.

Clients who tick boxes will never get out of the square.

It is the culture of a creative organisation (and brand-holding companies *must* be just that), which gives its people their strength and enables them to channel and fulfil their talents.

Great, transforming ideas come from confident cultures.

As the CEO of Britain's BBC once explained: "You can't make great television in an organisation that is depressed … the challenge is to make the organisation believe in itself."

Character is destiny in company culture. And confident cultures grow and feed off their own achievements.

It's said in academic circles that culture is like sex: it is impossible either to over- or under-emphasise it.

Yet a culture of fear, hurry-up-and-wait deadlines and armies of abominable no-men are just the start of the problems that a great and finely balanced idea must overcome, before it even gets the chance to do its work in the marketplace.

While the creative ego may appear strong to the casual observer, the idea itself is very vulnerable at the embryonic stage. Ideas are fragile things and can be carelessly crushed by a frown on the wrong person's face in a meeting. "Just the way someone puts down his tea cup … can paralyze creativity," *Gladiator* film composer, Lisa Gerrard, once explained.

Ideas are like tomatoes, it is said, easier to grow than to build.

An agency "CD," then, should also stand for Culture Director. Jamie Barrett is CD of San Francisco hothouse, Goodby Silverstein & Partners, and is responsible for growing some wonderful creative solutions from his sensitive plants.

Ideas that have grown into nice, plump, juicy profits for his clients.

THE LAW OF NICE BY JAMIE BARRETT

Before I begin my chapter on the Law of Nice, I have a couple confessions I need to make.

I'm as big an advertising jerk as the next guy.

There are hundreds of phone calls I still haven't returned; thousands of personal emails deleted without a response. I've ripped dozens of account people a new one, right to their face. And at one time or another, I've mocked probably every client I've ever had – behind their backs, of course.

The list of not-so-nice stuff I've done goes on. In fact, one of my most recent un-nice acts was promising to deliver this "Law of Nice" chapter four months ago, and then not delivering until today. Not particularly nice.

So as you read this, think of me not so much as the preacher who practises all this "nice" stuff, and more as a guy who believes in nice and wants to get better at it.

With that off my chest, I will now presume to be the guy who has the authority to talk about the importance — in advertising — of being nice.

Here's my thesis in a nutshell: When you're happy, you do your best work. And when you're a dick to people, on some level, you're probably not very happy.

Being happy in your work is important for another reason. Consider how much time we all spend doing this nuttiness we call advertising.

There are 168 hours in a week. Subtract 56 for sleep (eight hours a day). That leaves 112 waking hours. Now add up the weekends, the shortened vacations, the late nights, the trains, planes, rental-car shuttles and taxis, plus the time we all spend thinking or talking about work when we're not actually doing it, and I would conservatively guess that between half and two-thirds of your waking adult life will revolve around … advertising.

So I pose this question: why spend two-thirds of your life being a dick? Dicks in advertising are like anthrax. You don't want them to touch anyone, influence anyone, or be inhaled by anyone. When you have enough evidence of someone being a dick, clean the offender out of the office. Sterilise their chair and desk.

Being nice does not mean being a sugar-coating, feelings-sparing, half-truth-telling Pollyanna. But there are ways to deliver bad news or criticise that don't make people feel as worthless as a dotcom account. Work on your delivery. Find glimmers of positive in the negative. When you let people go, don't kick them out the door. Walk them out the door, and help them figure out the next door that makes sense for them.

Do dicks ever succeed? Temporarily, yes. I've heard Ed McCabe was a raging asshole, and he had a nice run. But I suspect Mr McCabe often looked to his left and right, saw a bunch of burnt bridges, and didn't feel particularly good about it. The desire to succeed is one of the most primal urges there is, but I would suggest that the desire to make a positive impact on the people around you is the most primal of all. And left unattended to, the whole success thing falls pretty flat.

In the end, no one will attend your funeral because you wrote a good catchphrase, or because you cashed in some stock options when your agency went public, or because you played politics better than someone else and got a promotion. Your greater legacy will be how people felt about you, not your work.

Of course, normally success and "niceness" go hand in hand. George Bush allegedly has handwritten tens of thousands of thank-you notes in his time. You may have your own issues with George, some not so positive. But you have to admit he is nice. And you have to also acknowledge that he "niced" his way all the way to the presidency of the United States.

Another great example of nice as a path to success comes from the world of sports. Did you know that Cal Ripken is a lifetime .277 hitter? For someone who is arguably the greatest baseball star of his generation, his numbers kind of suck. Granted, he is a great player, but I would argue that his fame and popularity are due as much, or more, to the fact that he is very simply a "nice guy." Jose Canseco, Ricky Henderson, Barry Bonds — all players with better stats, but all renowned jerks. Have you ever read an article about Bonds that didn't reference the fact that no one likes him?

There was a wonderful biography written about Ripken called *The Power of Nice*. And it's true, nice is a very powerful thing to be. It's true in life, it's true in baseball and it's true in advertising. Like any competitive business, advertising has its fair share of not-so-nice people. But if you think about it, that presents an opportunity for all the people who attempt to treat others well; who attempt to be nice.

It's the old advertising theory of cutting through the clutter. If there's a lot of "not-so-niceness" out there, "nice" will stand out that much more. It will "cut through" — a horribly cynical and manipulative way to look at things, but it's the hard truth. And hey, if you stand to gain something from being nice to people, what's the downside?

You may ask yourself why a Law of Nice is particularly relevant to the profession of advertising versus, say, accounting. Of course, treating people with decency ain't a bad policy no matter what your line of work. But I would argue that it is of even more critical importance in our line of work than it is in most.

Advertising is one of the most subjective occupations there is. It involves creativity, which is, in effect, personal expression. It's an expression of one's self; which means that every time a piece of work is evaluated, it is unavoidably personal. Egos are in the room. Feelings of self-worth. And because an ad's merits are ultimately hard to quantify, it becomes just one person's opinion versus another.

It's easier to tell someone they stocked a shelf wrong than to tell them their ideas are lame. I don't think there are more dicks in our profession, I just think the nature of our work brings out the dick in us more often than not. We need to be sensitive to that.

Are you a dick? It's worth asking yourself that. If your title is Executive-Global-Chief-Creative-Officer-Other-People-Do-The-Work-And-I-Take-Credit-For-It-Worldwide, then, yes, you probably are a dick.

But 99 times out of 100, the answer is no, you're not a dick. You may often act like a dick — we all do. But the key is to recognise the dick-like behaviour when it's starting to happen and, as quickly as possible, stuff it back in the dark corner of your brain from whence it sprang.

Niceness does have a nemesis, and its name is ego. Wanting to beat the other guy is as much a part of our makeup as wanting to get with the pretty (or handsome) receptionist. But both are biological urges we have to try and keep in check.

I like to try and think of advertising as a little like golf. Great golfers compete against the course. They don't stare at the scoreboard the whole round and obsess on their competitors; they stare at the shot in front of them and obsess on the best way to play it.

Apply the same thinking in your ad life. Don't waste energy comparing your work to the work of the guy down the hall, or the person with 20 page numbers after his name in the index of the One Show book. Waste your energy on creating your next great ad.

Chances are, there will be people who make advertising that is as or more celebrated than the work made by you. What's wrong with that? I say, prop up other talented people — in your agency and in other agencies. When you feel that heavy, petty jealousy feeling, ask yourself: Would you rather be in an industry that produces a ton of shit? I got into the creative side of this business because I was lucky enough to work across the hall from writers and art directors whose work inspired me. I tried to use that inspiration to fuel my own work. I still do.

Easier said than done, of course. If any creative person is being honest, they will admit this is incredibly hard. Imagine if all the great novelists worked on the same floor in the same building. Or all the great playwrights. Or the great screenwriters. The atmosphere would probably get a tad competitive.

But that's the way it is in a great advertising agency. Many of the best creatives in the world are asked to coexist and root for each other, even though some of them may be catching breaks and others may not. It's hard to be "nice" under these conditions. It's hard to be a team player. But the reality is, people will sense it if you're not. I know: I've lost friendships based on my inability to feel good about their success. So I keep reminding myself: The goal is to do well, not for others to do badly.

One last thought: No one is nice all the time. Okay, maybe Mr Rogers was. But even Fred, I suspect, had his moments of weakness when he berated King Friday for something, or instead of neatly hanging up his cardigan sweater, angrily threw it in the bottom of the closet.

My suggestion is, when you feel like tossing your cardigan, walk away instead. You probably work incredibly hard, and you deserve a break. Again, this is particularly hard in advertising. There are times when I would love to be a bank teller, or a tollbooth collector. Any job where I could walk away at the end of the workday and feel like there is nothing more I can do until I go to work again in the morning. This is clearly not the case in the business of creating ads. It's a 24-hour pursuit if you let it be.

Don't.

THE LORE OF NEGATIVITY

Marketers readily fall into rule worship. Faith can be blind. There are many false prophets. One of these was called "The Great God of Negativity" by some of the creative departments I've worked in.

This meant that their precious idea had been sacrificed on the altar by someone, on high, in the pecking order, who'd killed off the campaign by solemnly pronouncing it: "too negative."

Problem/Solution, most agree, is a powerful demonstration technique in any advertising medium.

The issue is, creative people love delving deep into the problem side of the equation and clients prefer the spotlight to be on the details of their products solution.

Why can't we be positive, the client high priest chants rhetorically? (After all, everyone knows the song says: "Ac-centuate the positive/Eliminate the negative.")

Leading Turkish clerics recently raised the same kind of question when it came to their country's rabid soccer fans. The clergy asked excited fans to stop swearing at matches and suggested, instead, they use expressions such as "Blessed Allah" or "Allah be praised" while watching football games.

Such phrases seem very worthwhile, of course, but perhaps they are not communicating the same thing as the profanities do; they don't quite capture the same the emotion, and indeed spirit, that the fans are feeling at the time.

There are many old wives beliefs about effective communication that should be defrocked.

David Ogilvy propagated the notion (since recanted) that humour doesn't work. He also preached that reversed out copy in print won't be read.

Charles Saatchi, founder of rival international networks Saatchi & Saatchi and later M&C Saatchi, debunked that when he produced his famous Health Department press ad that explained what happens in the moments after a fly lands on food: Long copy, white type, all *reversed out of a black background.*

Story goes that he actually had it set in both positive and reverse type. He plumped for the negative and the rest is history.

But, surely this very book is adding to the problem by pontificating about 22 so-called Laws? Well, hopefully readers will see these Laws as ingredients rather than formulas. (That's why the "And When to Violate Them" bit is in the title.)

They are designed not to contain, but ricochet.

An analogy might be music, which thrives (commercially) on new or original ways of reinterpreting a set of clearly identifiable, pre-existing notes. The chord sequence G, Em, Am, D7, for example, is the backbone of many hits from the doo-wop era through to pop; yet every song is individual and clearly differentiated to the market.

Then there's the 12 bar blues structure that underlies entire genres, from R&B to jazz, rock'n'roll to dance music.

Variations are infinite.

Ironically, there's another problem with ruling out negativity; that is, it can rule out the use of irony in your ads. And irony has been one of the most successful techniques in media for many years. Think *Seinfeld, The Simpsons, South Park* for a start.

The young get irony in the way that an older generation of clients often just don't. Irony is used as a way of making sure that others know that you know. It's cool code of a kind.

There's a positive tension in ambiguity, like Nike ironically using "ad buster" techniques. Nike successfully and humorously traded on ironic cynicism, even using the sweatshop allegations in cool ads.

Another irony is that some of the greatest campaigns ever written have been "negative." Jack Vaughan, an Australian Hall of Fame copywriter and former creative director of Y&R UK, has looked at the pluses and minuses to see whether this negative prejudice is really a positive thing in communication ... Or not.

THE LORE OF NEGATIVITY BY JACK VAUGHAN

It happened again the other day. A client objected to a headline I'd written that began with the word "Don't." The line was in the form of a question (another construct to which he objects), yet it had quite a positive point to make. But there the situation lay; as if some sacred rule had been broken and there was no avenue of appeal.

This negative taboo has been with us in advertising forever. I number it among the list of Top 10 unwritten laws many (but not all) clients seem to carry with them about ads. I'd love to know where they get them from, but they're precepts seemingly hardwired into so many of those who have anything to do with the commissioning or approval of advertising.

Other persistent beliefs are that the size, frequency or loudness of the product, brand name or logo is directly proportional to the ad's power to persuade, be remembered or to score highly on branding.

These are also, alas, untrue, as I've painfully found over years of creative practice, but they endure. I once made a spot for dog food that had the pack on screen the entire time, but failed to lift the branding score one jot.

The way to achieve high branding is to ... but that's another issue.

What's curious about *negaphobia* (a word I've just coined for this purpose) is that the belief is so damned tenacious when it comes to ads, but isn't so in any other sphere of life and language.

Even the expression "Let's not be negative" is, itself, negative — an entreaty to *not* do something. Yet it is the most natural and perfectly acceptable way of admonishing other people to not be defeatist, or to put it another way, to encourage them to stop being less than positive, which is in itself a negative (because merely saying, "Be positive" has a different meaning; more a sort of "have faith," "gird your loins" thing).

The same critics of creeping negativity in ads will feel totally comfortable, when on holidays, to buy a silly T-shirt with the words "NO WORRIES" or "DON'T WORRY, BE HAPPY" screened across it. These catchphrases are the very essence of our cultural mantras about feeling good. Not a problem, so to speak. Certainly, no complaints.

Similarly, it's high praise indeed when inviting someone to, for example, try a new wine vintage and they pronounce it, "Hey, not bad" especially if they add ... "not bad at all." In the same manner we say, "not too bad" in response to "How are you?" Or "not half bad" even though this could literally suggest "half of me (or it) *is* bad," or even "not just half bad, but totally bad."

Compared to these deliberate understatements, "quite good" or even "very good" can seem insipid. And "bad", of course, means *really* good in street parlance, as does "wickid" or "da bomb."

These highly useful, adverse forms of expression give our language power. A placard saying "CONTINUOUS PEACE" is not as powerful as one pleading "NO MORE WAR," which would be extremely positive if it were ever vaguely achievable.

Sometimes, it's literally a matter of life and death: "DON'T WALK," "WRONG WAY, GO BACK," "NO RIGHT TURN," "HIGH VOLTAGE, DO NOT TOUCH" are all difficult to say succinctly and powerfully in any positive construct.

There is even a whole category of English words called Negatives Without Positives, or Unpaired Words, like "dismayed" and "inept," "innocent" and "unscathed". They must have something going for them; their positive forms have largely become obsolete. Boringly positive things like "mayed" and "ept," "gruntled" and "kempt," didn't have the will to survive.

It's interesting that for years, at least in this country, incendiary materials were marked "INFLAMMABLE" or "HIGHLY INFLAMMABLE," possibly because the wrong negative prefix actually sounded more dire.

"Don't tell me!" means tell me everything. "You don't say!" means I really want you to say it, even though I can hardly believe what you're saying. As in, "Well, I *never.*"

The beauty of our language is the way you can stretch it.

Two negatives can be combined to make a positive: "You ain't seen nothin' yet."

The reverse is also true: I like the story about the linguistics professor who is lecturing that in no language can two positives create a negative. A sardonic voice calls out from the back of the hall: "Yeah, yeah". Similarly, "Yeah, right" has also taken on a completely opposite meaning.

In art school, we are often taught to draw or paint the "negative space," the areas of the scene that aren't the actual subject itself. Here, the negative helps our spatial perception to be fresh, quicker, more accurate.

And *chiaruscuro* – literally light and shade – help us see objects in the way we do, as planes and masses.

The trouble with *negaphobia* is that it locks up half our armoury. Negatives are powerful. "Why is this ad highlighting the problem?" the client will ask. Because it's less boring than the solution.

Why are newspapers full of bad news? Because people are much more interested in bad news; perhaps because it helps reassure them of how good they've got it. (There but for the grace of God.) That's why traffic crawls past car accidents.

It's also notable how in matters of romance or passion, the negative is often so vivid. I don't mean in the sense of the obvious: "Don't. Stop. Don't. Stop. Don't. Stop" … etc. I mean in many of the expressions we share with our beloved, often captured in popular music. "Never will I leave you," sounds more committed than "I will always stay," and "The 12th of Never" seems an even longer undertaking than the absolute "forever".

"Don't Worry Baby", from the mouths of the Beach Boys is quite reassuring. Gershwin ain't necessarily so negative in one of the anthems of *Porgy and Bess.* And when 10cc sing the haunting, "I'm Not in Love," you know they mean exactly the opposite: I'm denying being in love (and don't forget it) because I'm really so badly in love with you, I'll try any tactic to hang in there.

At the other end of the spectrum entirely, some of the most powerful words spoken in the history of the English language, by their arguably greatest deliverer, Churchill, are often nothing but negative. "Never has so much …," "We will not rest until …," "We will *never* surrender." Or even Kennedy's "Ask not what your ...". (We'll ignore Clinton's, "I did not have sex with ...".)

Those of a more academic bent than I have reached similar conclusions.

Googling around for references on "negative words", there are, of course, a hundred well-intentioned but predictable passages on how to eliminate negativity from your thoughts/life/writing/diary/relationship/emails/job, etc. (One earnest polemic on positivism carries the straight-faced headline: "Stop Being So Negative!").

A few, though, swim against the current created by the Hubbards and Carnegies with some interesting positive observations on negativity. French philosopher, Henri Bergson, author of *The Creative Mind* (1934), I learn, held that the world contains two opposing tendencies: the life force and the resistance of matter against that force. Kenneth Burke later built on this by examining the ethical implications of the negative. "No" and "Don't" are amongst the first words we learn as children: in the process learning not to throw our food on the floor or pull the dog's tail.

He goes further to suggest negativity is the very basis of human morality. (Eight of the Ten Commandments are "Shalt Nots").

Cognitive psychology research conducted by Tufts University professor Salvatore Scoraci has made advancements in understanding learning and "false memory" — mistaken recall of test words.

It was previously believed that memory was improved by "generative learning"; that people remember better when actively involved in forming an idea around, say, a particular word they're asked to memorise; the theory being that positive collaboration helped it stick.

Scoraci has found people are actually more likely to remember such words when given a negative cue than when given a positive one. This method of learning, using negative cues, is similar to how we find our way when we're driving our cars, *explains Scoraci.* If we make a wrong turn, we're much more likely to remember the correct route next time by remembering that we shouldn't go the wrong way again.

But to circle this back to advertising, my research has also revealed a fellow-sufferer and copywriter, Michael Gebert, in the US. (www.michaelgebert.com). In his online newsletter, *Shameless Self-Promotion,* Gebert echoes our frustrations:

NO COPYWRITER WILL ESCAPE THIS FATE. You write *a nice, punchy headline – "Nothing Fights Stains Like Splam-O." Then the comment comes back: "Nothing" is negative. Can't we turn it into a positive? (Like what? "Splam-O Fights Stains Better Than Things"?)*

Gebert goes on to say: *Put a sentence with a "not" or a "don't" in it in front of those people, and suddenly, they'll be impressed by the mystical power of that one single word to repel all customers, regardless of the actual meaning of the sentence. That's not grammar. It's voodoo.*

What's most confounding to me about this whole issue is that some of the most negative expressions have long been the very stock-in-trade of the world of hard sell. How many products have declared themselves "Not your ordinary ..." or "Not for everybody" to boost their desirability to many? "Accept no substitute," "Don't buy till you try our ...," "Will not be undersold". "Nobody comes close to our ...". Just as the much-imitated "Drive away, no more to pay" has recently become.

There are also plenty of specific brands with famous and successful campaigns based on seemingly negative thoughts:

"Lemon" or "It's ugly, but it gets you there" were never going to be taken literally about Volkswagen, but said a lot about their cleverly self-effacing attitude. That, along with "You don't have to be Jewish" for Levy's bread, more or less started modern, more candid advertising.

More recently, "I never read the Economist. (Management trainee, aged 42)" has helped put that magazine high up the racks. The Wallpaper Institute of America claims, "Nothing gets your attention like wallpaper," along with whimsical visuals. The *Village Voice* has been honest and successful by declaring its individuality with "Not America's favourite paper" (and thus yours).

When Eveready Batteries themes their ads "Never say Die," it's far more declarative than "Always stay alive." Heineken, in the UK, sold a lot of beer that "Refreshes the parts other beers cannot reach." And there's no other line like David Jones', at least in Australian retail. As Michael Gebert says, the arguments against the yea-sayers are obvious: *"So obvious that they always get the same response: 'Yeah, I know. But change it, wouldja? It's just one word.'"*

Anti-negativity, he claims, *"deprives a writer of one of the most effective rhetorical devices in the English language, for no good reason. Would GM still own the car market if only they'd said, "You Would Really Rather Drive a Buick?" Would the James Bond movies have been even more successful if they'd had titles like "Dr. Yes" and "Tomorrow Always Lives"?*

I couldn't agree more. Or should I say, I agree as much as possible.

I've always thought that Sara Lee's long–running campaign in the US, "Nobody Doesn't Like Sara Lee" was so much more charming and approachable than the overblown self-congratulation of it's underlying sentiment, "Everybody Loves Sara Lee." It's a tradition that goes back to "Nothin' says lovin' like somethin' from the oven" for Duncan Hines cake mixes. Or was it Pillsbury?

And what could've been more compelling than the theme that carried American Express to world popularity, "Don't Leave Home Without It." Would it have conveyed the same indispensability expressed as"Always take it with you when you leave home"?

I think not.

But then, maybe I'm just being negative.

THE LAW OF EXECUTION

I magine the movie *Casablanca* with Ronald Reagan (who was cast originally) instead of Humphrey Bogart. Or *Mission Impossible* without Lalo Shiffren's iconic theme music.

My point is there's occasionally a little something in the execution or production that really adds to a basic idea, improves/changes/replaces it, and literally makes all the difference to its success.

Maybe it was suggested by the commercial's director, or ad-libbed by an actor on the set, or by the muso on the last day of recording, or inspired by the catering lady. Not only can an idea come from anywhere, it can arrive anytime and from anyone. Sometimes it's these grace notes that actually create the "burr" that hooks people to a campaign.

Which begs the question of when an advertising idea is finished?

Usually, once the client has bought it, an idea remains stillborn at that level in its development. How else can it be controlled? Business loves being in control; sometimes more than it loves being successful.

Kotler's view of marketing, adopted by advertising planners everywhere, is rooted in the notion of control: analysis, planning, implementation and measurement.

It's also true that many rational businesspeople aren't comfortable with creativity; many would rather stick with plans made in meetings, where everything is spelled out in advance and all new ideas are firmly in hand.

Ambiguity is not tolerated for long. This leads management to gravitate towards the familiar, to premature conclusions, to impose clichés and stereotypes. Which, in turn, is why so many ads just seem like the brief committed to film. That is committing a crime against effectiveness.

Meanwhile, the unpredictable way that consumer desires and creativity actually match up in the marketplace continues to disturb and baffle businesspeople

Truth is, for it to be successful, an advertising idea must translate and transcend the logic of the marketing.

How, then, do you allow for the possibility of improvement in the execution of your advertising idea? *Kaizan* is the Japanese word meaning "continuous improvement." Apply it to your advertising and the idea should get noticeably better from concept to final script, from storyboard to director's treatment, and from first cut to final client presentation.

Better and better, layer by layer.

Great advertising needs a "conspiracy of good intentions" among everybody involved in the process.

Our next contributor believes in advertising as a collaborative art. He even has a central creative area where his agency work-in-progress is displayed, so everyone passing may express their views on it.

Different ads become great at different times. A great proposition or script is a start. But a script is not an ad. An ad may only become great after the editor gets his hands on it, or the casting agent makes an inspired choice, or the photographer works magic.

All of these stages should be considered as part of the creative process, not as part of the agency˜– client presentation process.

The greatness should be allowed to sneak out at any time.

Irish-born Mike O'Sullivan has worked in the UK and Australasia, and as creative director of New Zealand's world famous Colenzo/BBDO, he has tried to *reverse engineer* great ideas through execution.

It's an insight into how many creative people actually create: Execution first. Idea second.

Produced great advertising this way he has.

THE LAW OF EXECUTION BY MIKE O'SULLIVAN

This chapter is about the Law of Idea and Execution, and the difference between them. And, more importantly, which one should come first.

Writing about ideas is pretty tricky as we all define an idea differently. As a result, quite a few people will disagree with this law; in fact, a lot of you may not even understand it.

The law of accepted wisdom states that art directors and copywriters (hereafter referred to as "the creatives") conceive an advertising idea, then go about executing the idea. In layman's terms, they come up with a common theme, then create different TV, billboard and radio scenarios. For example, a TV campaign may have four different ads with different actors, locations and dialogue, but there will be a common theme running throughout. This "theme" is usually the idea.

An idea is a medium or property that communicates a product benefit in an extraordinary way. In other words, it will often dramatise a boring fact through words, pictures or sound.

The best ideas tend to be the simple ones.

They are the ones the punter looks at and gets straight away.

One of the great advertising "truths" is that creatives should be able to write a good idea on a postage stamp or napkin. Another common belief is that you should be able to explain an idea in a sentence. Below are a few examples from history.

Idea: People react with huge surprise when they see unbelievably cheap VW prices
Executions: Show various people seeing VW prices with extreme reactions, e.g. A woman feels faint or a dentist mentions a price to make a patient open his mouth further.
Endline: "Surprisingly ordinary prices"

Idea: Australians love their XXXX more than their wives, cars, life itself, etc.
Execution: An Aussie bloke still reaching for a can of XXXX whilst nearly fully consumed by an alligator.
Endline: Australians wouldn't give a XXXX for any other beer

Idea: John Smiths is a no bullshit beer for no bullshit blokes.
Execution: John Smiths drinker climbs to top of Olympic-style diving board and does a "bomb"
Endline: No nonsense

Idea: The taste of real oranges is a huge taste hit
Execution: To demonstrate the hit of real oranges, a person gets a smack on the face from a big orange bloke every time he takes a sip of Tango.
Endline: You know when you've been tangoed

All of the campaigns above have several executions. In fact, when a person picks up what a campaign idea is, they can usually come up with their own executions.

Not all ideas can be summed up in words, but most of the goods one can. This is why billboards with headlines are pretty popular in our business.

For the last few years I've been creative director of an ad agency called Colenso BBDO in New Zealand. New Zealand is a small country with small marketing departments and small budgets.

This "smallness" is great for ideas.

It has made our industry, my agency and I work in a different way. It has forced our clients, planners and suits to stick to one proposition, one benefit. The creative work has to be simple. There is no choice.

We can't write mediocre scripts and throw a million-dollar director at it. Nor can we just come up with a crap headline and shoot the visual in Florence.

In truth, we have to come up with simple, affordable, easy-to-produce ideas.

An example. Our client TV3 is the second biggest network in NZ. A junior creative team comes to me with ideas to promote their upcoming TV premiere of the movie *Scream*. They suggest putting red dye into the water fountain in Custom Street, Auckland (the NZ equivalent of Piccadilly Circus).

The client said yes. The cost of the dye and street painting came to less than $800. The media coverage in the newspapers comes to about $500,000.

Idea first, then execution, very much second.

A creative team will come up with an idea, script and present it. The client approves it, then it's "By hook or by crook," where we'll do anything to get it made. In extreme cases an agency copywriter might act, or a client do voice over. Whatever it takes.

Understandably, this way of producing ads affects how we conceive ads. I've noticed this particularly through being presented to as a creative director. Nearly all of the creative teams I've worked with, present their TV/print/radio in the same way.

Most of the time they present their idea in a sentence, then they list off the executions. Nobody walks in with a film clip or a piece of Dutch animation because on nearly every occasion we can't afford it. So quite often, the "thought" or "idea" has to be original in words, not necessarily how it looks or sounds.

Now this law has been pretty good to us and any other creative who practises it. As an agency, we've retained business, won business and picked up our fair share of Lions.

End of story?

Well no, not really. Having practised this law and benefited hugely from it, I can now tell you it's crap. Well not crap, but certainly flawed.

I'm beginning to believe *a great execution is more important than the idea.* By that I mean the funny, clever picture, sound effect bit during any ad, may well be better than the big creative idea behind it. Punters like to laugh, they don't really give a toss what the ad idea is.

We've all heard a good retail ad penned by the local plumbing shop or hardware store. Often it's some dumb gag, without a clear single-minded thought.

The thing is, though, that modern advertising training and methodology says we should have a "logical, clever bit."

I first noticed this in radio. You can come up with a great idea, which just doesn't work on radio. If the ad's not funny, touching or dramatic, you're stuffed.

A couple of years ago, one of our teams were working on a poster brief for Casio Mini TV. They came into my office and showed me a "Cannes style" ad. (We called them "Cannes style" because there appears to be certain style of ad that regularly wins at the festival. In print, they tend to have a full-page visual with a pack shot — usually a bit too small — bottom right. Underneath the pack shot is a line with either the proposition, e.g. the powerful light bulb, hottest chilli, or an explanation of the visual.)

Show Ads

I laughed out loud when I saw this campaign, then I blew the ads out.

They didn't make sense to me. It just said Mini TV. I asked them to do more work explaining the benefit of a Casio Mini TV.

A day later I changed my mind. I was being too logical.

The benefit/idea was in the name. I initially reacted the way punters do, in that I laughed. That's what it's all about.

That's why Cannes is one of the better ad awards. A lot of the TV work that wins tends to be visually stunning or just plain hilarious. The jury tends to award stuff the way a punter would.

The way advertising briefs are researched, composed and presented is half the problem.

A creative person gets a brief with a written proposition. He or she will sit at their desk and think and play with those words. Those words will lead to sentences, which then lead to pictures. This process will lead he or she to a certain style of ad. A few of these ad styles are below.

Demonstration:
This is where the product is shown working for real
e.g. cooking pot used to melt inferior cooking pot.

Hyperbole demonstration:
This is where the benefit is still a demonstrational but done in an unreal way
e.g. VW: Surprisingly ordinary prices; a mouse running on a steering wheel to demonstrate easy car steering.

Analogy:
Used when you are unable to show the subject matter. A good example is when one small company wants to say it's as good as bigger companies in the market. The mouse scaring elephant scenario is an oft-used solution for this.

What I'm trying to say is that every creative goes through the same process everyday. Our thinking is linear, our solutions systematic. Why do you think we regularly come up with an ad somebody else has done? We get the same brief and our system comes up with the same solutions.

I believe truly great work happens when you mess with the system. Throw a spanner into the creative works.

NZ Skier is a good case of a screw up in the system. The client had no money so the creatives were told to they had use stock photography. This setback turned out to be a godsend. We were forced to come up with a good idea, because the visual was decided.

Another example happened recently to me. I was doing some ads with a junior team on a video game called *Mortal Kombat*. It's an ultra violent fighting game with various muscle-clad characters beating the shit out of each other.

One day while thinking about it, I laughed out loud. We were thinking it would be funny if these guys were really a bit soft and girly. We did a test using two of these animated characters. One was asking the other out of for a coffee because he felt that "they needed to discuss their differences."

One of the copywriters, Richard Maddocks, ad-libbed the dialogue with a funny, high-pitched voice, while Ben, our designer did some coarse animation.

It was funny, but it didn't have an ending. Then we thought maybe the characters should have a fight to end the ad. We did that and it was still funny.

Now all we needed was an idea.

We spent a day coming up with the idea and a line to summate the ad. The ads ended up being about these guys trying to talk but always ending up fighting. We wrote three ads featuring the guys initially talking, but no matter how hard they tried, they always ended up having a fight.

The end line was "Violence. Always the best solution."

We started off with a sight gag, ended on a campaign idea.

Execution Idea.

Now this wasn't a great campaign, but it showed a changed in our order of thinking. Some of the truly great ads of our time have been reverse engineered.

I don't believe "Wassup" came from a three-page brief. I doubt a creative guy jumped out of his office chair and shouted "Why don't we have these four blacks guys talking to each other?"

Most creative directors would never buy that ad based on a script. It's common knowledge the execution was there well before the idea. The "Cog" ad for Honda or the brilliant Club 18-30 campaign were hardly devised without some executional inspiration.

Advertising history has countless campaigns based on existing visual material and techniques. UK advertising owes a lot to UK sitcoms, movies and skit shows. Many campaigns have been devised around their formats or star characters. During the 1990s most London creatives could count on a Harry Enfield or Paul Whitehouse character to deliver a client's benefit.

This is not a new way of working. But it is a way that could be developed into something greater.

It may sound mad, but what if every brief forced you to work back from the execution?

What if creatives were given a relevant visual/audio stimulus that they must include as part of their solution? It could be a great comedy sketch or a piece of poetry.

What if you were given a creative brief for a mobile phone that said you had to feature a banana in your TV script? Maybe a magazine ad for a car that couldn't show the car, or could only feature its nearest competitor in the visual.

All of these suggestions immediately change the thought process.

Ultimately I believe the Law of Idea and Execution should be broken. Now, when I'm writing or judging ads, I force myself and my teams to break the law.

It can be anything from putting in an executional mandatory, like using a stock shot to using a soundtrack that fits the brand. If they present something that's funny but doesn't fit with the brand, then we try and make it fit.

As much as I can, I'll abandon the logical route, because execution is about emotion.

It's laughter, tears, tension, drama, etc.

Logical people will find it hard to work this way, but the chances are, it will make your ads better.

THE LAW OF EVOLUTION

F our of the most potent words in the advertising universe used to be "As seen on TV."

How quickly things change.

Media fragmentation is making advertising choices increasingly complex, with current predictions indicating that there may be fewer than 10 to 15 years left in which to establish a global or national brand the traditional way.

In the US, free-to-air TV audiences are falling constantly (though networks are charging more and more to reach them) and it's now ideas bigger than the borders of traditional advertising that are the pointy end of marketing.

The Law of Evolution is not about the survival of the fittest, but the most adaptable. Sheer media muscle is no longer enough, Mr Dinosaur.

Every campaign should attempt to step outside the traditional media boxes that have to be ticked.

Look for ideas by thinking about your target person's total time, not just their media time. When are they really in the right frame of mind to listen, as opposed to when the advertiser wants to talk?

Advertiser mindsets have to move away from the cosy pigeon-holing of consumers into age or socio-groups, and move toward a more realistic assessment of people's real-life attitudes and aspirations.

This book exists because things have changed so much in the advertising world; we're trying to ground our thinking in the most fruitful earth, regardless of the marching mutability of the times.

So what can be relied upon in the future, apart from more change?

In my den, I keep a map of the globe that, along with the dry land masses, shows the topography of the ocean floor. When you see exposed all the underwater chasms, peaks, channels and plains that are usually hidden beneath the surface of the waves, then the flow of the gulf streams, the reflux of the oceans, and the patterns of the world's weather are all far more easily comprehended.

Unfortunately, there is no analogous map available that can indicate the various subtle depths and undercurrents in today's communication.

However, we do have some brilliant navigators, like David Lubars, the Fallon US creative director, who collected Cannes' inaugural Titanium award in 2003 for the agency's groundbreaking campaign for BMW.

The future seems clear: evolve or dissolve.

THE LAW OF EVOLUTION BY DAVID LUBARS

A fascinating paradox about advertising people: we passionately push clients to be open to change, yet we're the least open to change ourselves. The most obvious example of this is what's going on today with new mediums and technology.

Advertising people are not facing the fact that, in a few short years, the 30-second commercial will no longer be *the* medium, but simply *a* medium.

Consider. By the end of 2003, 30 million US households will have broadband, and by 2006, 45% of all viewing will be on demand.

This means lots of people will be watching exactly what they want and not watching what they don't. Today, we're seeing a vast erosion of network ratings. We're also seeing a disproportionate increase in the use of TiVo-like devices (I've had a TiVo since 1999 and I admit to happily zipping through the annoying commercials).

Yet, advertising agencies desperately cling to the 30 seconds. They hope all this new medium and technology stuff will go away. Or, if they've been around a while, they hope they can keep doing what they're doing until they retire, leaving it for the next generation to figure out. Unfortunately, this isn't going away, because viewers love the power and control they now have.

So, to me, there are two choices: think differently or be flushed down the 20th-century toilet. That's not just my opinion either. Last year, *USA Today* identified a new group of teens-to-twenties they call the "Unreachables" — people who are almost impossible to touch through the mainstream mediums. And, recently, when Sun Microsystems' marketing director was asked why he fired his agency of only three years, he answered, "The big agencies only think about doing the next 30 spot."

The good news in all this is that the new technology and media developments offer an extraordinary, never-seen-before opportunity for creativity — the very thing agencies thrive on. Open-minded, big-thinking people will kick ass in this new world. Some already are. Our agency's BMW films are a good example. The films were designed to solve a simple but shattering problem for our client: our target was no longer watching enough TV to be reached effectively; we couldn't show him the cars properly.

We sat and thought about it. We knew this person spent 10 or 12 hours a day at work. We knew he had a powerful computer on his desk. The logic was, "Why not visit him where he is — at the computer?" The client saw the value in the idea immediately and signed on. There were risks involved, for sure, like figuring out how to make a long-form film. But the idea was sound; we figured it out. The client initially expected three million views. By summer 2003, they hit 50 million views. BMW has also had the best US sales year in its history, in the midst of an extremely tough economy. Going beyond ads seems to have worked well for them.

Another example is our successful launch for the Archipelago stock exchange, which featured *The Open Show*, a minute-long TV show that ran every day at 7:59 a.m. — right before the conventional

Madonna

Car Jumping

Don C.

Clive from *Ticker*

James Brown & Gary Oldman

BMW Films. 50 million views and counting. In 2002, BMW experienced the best US sales in its history.

stock market opened at eight. Another is our Buddy Lee Challenge, which brought huge numbers of kids to the brand through a video game we designed.

Look, I'm not saying commercials are going to go away. They'll always exist; we'll always produce great spots. What I am saying is, commercials are going to be a smaller part of the mix; they're going to be somewhat marginalised. That's why we're evolving Fallon to another place. It's been great for our clients and for us.

What!

Beauty Contest

Cannon

Mullet Guy

Town Crier 1

Lisa

Archipelago. *The Open Show* introduced a new way of trading stocks in a hugely successful, and funny, way.

We will continue to embrace new ideas and put our clients in a category of one rather than in the field of sameness their competitors play in. It's been fun, stimulating, rewarding and successful. Plus, there's that little thing about it being the path to survival. Darwin wrote something about that.

Karate Stance

Roy Getting Lasered

Electric Eel

Curry

Challenge Title

Supergreg

Lee Dungarees. The Buddy Lee character invited kids to play an online game to win cool prizes. The secret clues you needed to win the game were printed inside the pockets of dungarees.

THE OUTLAW

S panish Nobel Literature Laureate and poet, Juan Ramon Jimenez, said: "If they give you ruled paper, write the other way."

Welcome to the Law of the Outlaw.

Differentiation is the reason for a brand's existence.

Differentiation is, therefore, the basic responsibility of a brand's advertising.

So why do so many ads look the same? Especially, as Jim Aitchison says: "The less an ad looks like an ad, the more likely it is to get noticed."

If everyone is zigging, and following certain prescribed rules, then the only sensible thing to do is to zag.

Be a contrarian.

An outlaw.

"I have no use for rules, they rule out the brilliant exception," said the great Ed McCabe, himself the most disciplined of copywriters.

Can any or all of the Laws in this book be broken and successful advertising still created?

For that matter, if one applied all the Laws in

this book, wouldn't that necessarily transgress at least one of them?

Like any workmanlike craft, you have to learn the rules before you know how to bend them; but the Outlaw is not about mere rebellion.

Every category has its own set of unwritten advertising conventions on how it should look. It takes a brave client to break out, but that's what you have to do to stand out.

If every law in this book *were* actually adhered to in the commercial world, then the Law of the Outlaw would become the most important.

But who in their right mind would want to violate The Law of Selling? Well, sometimes it is not retail sales that are imperative, but corporate objectives or "pure" brand issues; but, surely, there must always be a direct causal connection between those strategies and selling something in the immediate, foreseeable instance, even if it is only a notion or an emotion?

Can you violate The Law of Simplicity and still succeed? Perhaps, would be the honest answer, but it costs big money and a relentless disregard for basic professionalism. It's one Law I would never break intentionally, and still expect a good ROI.

How about The Law of Positioning? Violate it at your utmost peril I think.

What about The Law of Relevance?

Borrowed interest is a valid creative technique, but unless the ultimate "point" of the ad is relevant to the market or massages their feelings, well, what is the point? You can do it, but you won't succeed.

The Law of Humour? If being funny makes your product more interesting, empathetic, cool or memorable, then don't be scared of being light-hearted. Even in heavy-hearted categories, like funeral parlours, humour can be appropriately disarming and down-to-earthily human.

It used to be said that nobody buys from a clown; these days, nobody buys from a bore.

The Law of Disruption? Break it and blend in; hardly sensible.

The 19th-century English artist and thinker, John Ruskin, used to encourage people to draw the world around them. Not to teach them how to draw, rather to teach them about the world.

How to see.

How to notice, rather than to merely look.

This book, in a way, is an attempt to do that for advertising. By studying and drawing on these "Laws", the reader will find a new way to see advertising. And discover ways to make advertising that is noticed, not merely looked at.

MT Rainey, who built a marvellously successful UK agency through championing planning, has made a career from knowing the rules and knowingly breaking with accepted notions.

Here, she lays down the philosophy of the Outlaw.

It stands and delivers.

THE OUTLAW BY MT RAINEY

To paraphrase the late great Peter Cook, everything we've just told you is a lie, including this.

Assuming you are reading this chapter last (but of course you're not, you're an outlaw) the Escher-like trope of this book must have been amply demonstrated by now, i.e. the application of laws to an endeavour which depends for its success on the breaking of them.

When originally asked to contribute a chapter, I not only bridled at the title, but in an attempt to comply I struggled for weeks to identify any law of advertising, other than "sods," to which I could sign up publicly and with impunity.

Sods Law in advertising is of course that which says: *When you have just come up with a brilliant idea, sold it to the client and are about to go into production, a competitor will immediately publish the said idea in an executional form far inferior to that which you had envisaged, causing you to go back to the drawing board from whence you came, with the deadline from hell.*

Being the tight-arsed pedant that I am, I was not wont to submit to generalisations like humour, emotion or simplicity in the pursuit of a "law" of advertising, and indeed others here have sensibly, usefully and certainly much better than I could have, outlined the wisdom of those great truths of advertising, among others.

But I, dear reader, opted out, copped out and frankly chickened out and suggested the title of this chapter. I had some temporary difficulty persuading Michael that the title should be "The Outlaw" and not "The Law of the Outlaw" before I realised that, in spite of the challenging aperture, I was fast disappearing up my own rear end.

This chapter will not be long. In many ways the point is made by the title and it's position in the book. Perhaps a summary of the book's intent and perhaps a "full stop" to the arguments within. It is exactly the same point as Michael makes in his introduction and that I'm sure many of my fellow contributors have made in one way or another in their respective chapters. It is naturally about the folly of formulas, the rejection of rules and the shame of the same. It has of course to do with the requirement to "think different," the necessity to "break the rules" and the desirability of "disruption," Advertising has always employed the rhetoric of the outlaw and its greatest practitioners and proselytisers, from Ray Rubicam through Bill Bernbach to Jean Marie Dru, have always preached a form of subversion.

And if I have any tacit knowledge after 25 years in the business (I started young), it would be genuinely summarised by endorsing that polemic and leaving it at that.

There are, however, a number of nuances that I would like to add, partly by way of reinforcement, and partly because the changing context for creativity and ideas in the endeavour loosely known as advertising, seems more than ever to demand that we think differently and to defend our stance in doing so.

Much as we may love the Clint Eastwood imagery, The Outlaw is of course not a person. It's not the mad genius with The Tindersticks CDs in the corner office of the creative department. Neither is it simply a process, though there are legitimate processes which may arise from it. And it is definitely not a positioning, a posture or a pose available only to a few preternaturally trendy agencies for a finite period of time (though in the absence of serious competition in the US throughout the 1980s, Chiat/Day flew the Pirate flag for a very long time). It's not just something that every agency should *have* or every agency should *do*. As a blueprint for creative thinking, "The Outlaw" is a *mentality* and a belief system that should permeate our industry and inspire everyone in it, if we are to continue to be valuable and valued.

Because of course, as Ed McCabe said, creativity remains the last competitive weapon, the last legal means by which one company may gain unfair advantage over another. Information technology, the globalisation of the market economy, the liberalisation of markets, the fragmentation of media, and the shift of Western consumerism towards experience - and desire-based drivers and away from needs-based drivers, all contribute to the rise in importance of "intangibles" and the primacy of creativity, coupled of course with the ability to apply it as a primary asset of businesses and organisations today.

When I worked in the States in the eighties, I was struck by the open acknowledgement, even by some practitioners, that there were two kinds of advertising: creative advertising and "advertising that sells," whereas in Britain the creative imperative was widely accepted at the time. I think that since then things have changed for the better in the States, but in these recent straitened times in all of our markets, in which some companies clearly still see creativity as a luxury, the reality is that more than ever The Outlaw mentality is not an option — it is a mandate.

In fact arguably, there is no other industry in which creativity in its broadest sense (which would encompass innovation and even boldness) is such an absolute prerequisite as it is in advertising. In many other industries which employ creative skills, innovation and creativity are only a part of the product mix. The film industry, while producing highly creative and innovative new films, is also openly enslaved by a successful formula. Similarly, the music industry churns out endless "best ofs" and compilations alongside the genuinely new bands and albums. Architects, software developers, game designers — have a leading edge and a bleeding edge, but all also have genuine "markets" for the familiar and the tried and trusted. In other aspects of culture, I may appreciate and thrive on the new and the different (or I may not), but I will certainly at least some of the time be comforted, reassured and entertained by the familiar, in fact often by the identical. This self evidently can't be said of advertising at least in principle.

Actually I think it's less about "in principle" and more about "in theory." People consume music, film, games, etc. in an open and active marketplace. They exchange money for them and exert choices and preferences for them. They do not "consume" advertising in the same way – although it exists in the same cultural space — and of course we use this term (to consume) to describe what people do with advertising.

This, while being the bleeding obvious, is at the heart of the creative imperative for advertising and is often overlooked. Like other aspects of culture, advertising of course operates in the public sphere, but unlike other aspects of culture it is compelled to intrude and will only effectively be "consumed" if it succeeds in doing so in some way. It makes sense then that the *sine qua non* of any advertising is to get noticed. Now here's the science part. In purely neurological terms, the brain *notices what's different* and relegates or files away the familiar. Suddenly, "resist the usual" becomes less of a folksy slogan than an astonishingly compelling summary of Pattern Recognition and Signal Detection Theory, and at least two important and established scientific fields are clearly seen to support The Outlaw mentality for Advertising.

But will this model of advertising survive much longer? Is it surviving now in the cold climate of the early 20th century recession, in the multichannel digital world? When does The Outlaw become The Outcast?

One of the most gleeful and persistent predictions of the last 10 years has been that of the death of mass media and of advertising. In fact in the firmament of marketing services as a whole, advertising is now pretty much the business that dares not speak its name. It is deeply unfashionable these days to be optimistic about advertising but I'm afraid I really am.

I once made a speech at a creative awards show in Australia in the zenith of the dotcom boom, which I called Crystal Bollocks. It was basically a humanistically based rant against the ridiculous, unrealistic predictions of what was going to happen to consumer behaviour and therefore to mass media and advertising as a result of the internet. It seemed to me and others (though not many of them were vocal at the time) that the market was being completely inflated by confusing the possible with the probable, and assuming that the essential nature of consumers was to be highly rational and highly individualistic. The consumer was basically a value-seeking missile operating alone. In spite of the frenzy of optimism and excitement it created at the time, the imagery conjured of the future was actually highly dystopian. Taken to it's *logical* conclusion, it was positively "Vulcanic."

Billions of individuals tapping interminably away at their PCs, reading The Daily Me, ordering more of the same of everything, giving brands they knew and liked occasional permission to send them a new brochure. Having perfect information at their fingertips, people would endlessly and tirelessly use it to make comparisons and would, therefore, make highly rational "perfect" choices. Stuck in a turn-of-the-century time warp in which novelty, serendipity and discovery had no place, they would never do anything as quotidian as visit shops or read books or watch TV. There would be no such thing as mass media, no such thing as broadcast and little occasion for shared media experiences as people endlessly "interacted" with programming or entertainment in real time. Certainly they would not be passive consumers or even receivers of advertising, as they would naturally want to edit that out. Their world would be entirely on-demand and customised. And boring, and predictable, and isolated, and of course as it turns out, deeply unlikely.

This vision of the future consistently ignored the social nature of being human and the herd or tribal instinct of the individual human being. It also completely underestimated the hedonics of the physical browsing and shopping experience and underestimated the ability of conventional retailers to innovate towards this. It dismissed the entire foundation of the entertainment industry, i.e. that the vast majority of entertainment is lean back not lean forward, because people like it that way. It ignored one of the driving features of the market economy as defined by Adam Smith, that one of the primary functions of wealth is the display of wealth, and that therefore we must have a shared understanding of what the signifiers of wealth are, i.e. brands and brand values and images. And it also forgot why brands evolved in the first place — to make choice more simple in an oversupplied, overchoiced world.

Five years later, the bubble burst and while many of the frantically predicted effects of the internet are now happening more slowly but for real, they are largely creating shifts in the balance and mix of people's behaviour rather than changing it completely. While mass market ratings have declined as a percentage of the whole, TV advertising both here in the UK and in the US is more in demand and sold for more of a premium than ever. There are still many shared media experiences and we still have water cooler (or pub or chat room) conversations about ads and programmes because of course they are part of our shared culture. The power of good television advertising, in particular to work broadly over a population and quickly in time, is still dramatically demonstrated everyday by tracking study results. There are, however, also wonderful new opportunities in other media and in using media and the mix of media differently that are now available which, when The Outlaw mentality is applied, give us even more chances to innovate, add value and have fun doing it.

Creativity and The Outlaw mentality are still necessary for the science of advertising to work as most of it still works on the push model and much of it always will. Creativity is even more necessary than ever now though as complexity increases as networks of connections, influences and channels multiply, as people's experience dissects their image of things in more and more ways at more and more points. Being creative in how you communicate is a much, much more weighty responsibility when " everything communicates." People's experience of things in general and brands in particular is highly impressionistic rather than highly opinionated. It is also constantly changing and evolving relative to other brands in contexts which we cannot know or control. Jeremy Bullmore uses the lovely image of a bird building a nest from twigs and found objects to describe this. A similar argument runs through the work of Seth Godin and Malcolm Gladwell, that, in this interconnected world, the most important and powerful communication about a brand is that between customers and other customers, rather than that which happens between a brand and its customers.

Communication and specifically advertising has never simply been about the paint job at the end of the production line, but these days that way of thinking, that way of using creativity is positively dangerous.

In fact, there is one law that I think may be worth codifying at this point and that's the "Law of Unintended Consequences." It is no longer possible to simply measure the effects of our intended messages on our intended target, and trade off "conversion" against "wastage." We need to understand that any action will have an impact on all recipients and that the negative impact may be as powerful an influence on the many as the positive is on the few. Why is it still OK for the direct marketing industry to propose that a 3% response rate is a good thing if it can be proved to be cost effective? What about the 97% you bored, insulted, misunderstood, inconvenienced or angered in order to achieve it? A similar argument might be made about advertising which seeks to shock or pander, or indeed advertising which clearly creates a promise which bears no relations to people's actual experience of the brand.

So the challenges for marketing are far more complex now and therefore the requirement to harness creativity throughout the process is clearly there. Our industry understands creativity better than most because it has been an imperative for us for so long. We know how to foster, use, manage and reward creativity. We accommodate The Outlaw mentality, whereas many client cultures would find it alien and the organism would tend to expel it. The way of thinking that might be termed The Outlaw Mentality, so prized in our culture, should then be even more valued by our clients. And yet there is a sense in which we are our own worst enemy in this industry; by seeking to become more like them by being seen to be more driven by rationality and accountability when in fact we should be helping them to be more like us. The two are not incompatible at all. They are just different parts of the whole. As Bob Dylan once said, "Only an honest man can live outside the law."

So you will have to decide ultimately for yourself whether you think "The Outlaw," and therefore the theme of this book, is a curmudgeon's manifesto, the hopeless last chirps of a dying signal, or whether it is a defiant defence of a proud and relevant tradition that is in danger of being "outcast" by the Philistines. As ever the truth is imprisoned in a cliché. Whatever you think, think different.

THE LAW OF DEADLINES

B rands are the response to the advertiser's life and death struggle to differentiate in a white-hot world of competition, where the new and latest can go stone cold in what seems like hours.

On one side of the problem, you can mould the kind of culture where everybody comes in *on time* and gets the idea out *in time* — all work done, finished and despatched on the due date.

But the reality is you can still end up with a lousy piece of tripe as an ad.

And you'll fail; right on schedule.

Desk time, face time, is not the same as effective time.

(It's the same with dichotomy with budgets; as Titanic producer, Jon Landau, once said: "Nobody remembers a bad movie that came in under budget.")

On the other hand, "I love the whooshing sound they make as they pass," is how the humorist Douglas Adams once spoke of deadlines.

Oscar Wilde would have agreed.

He inspired many agency creatives with his quote: "I spent the morning inserting a comma and I whiled away the afternoon removing it."

However, history shows that while the big don't always eat the small, the fast always eat the slow.

So, while it's true that inspiration doesn't always materialise right on schedule, the uncompromising speed-to-market ethos means the immutable Law of the Deadline is the ultimate reality; break this law, and you can expe...

THE 10 IRRESPONSIBLE CRIMES AGAINST ADVERTISING

(THAT ALWAYS VIOLATE PROFITS)

As in the real world, there are more crimes committed in Adland than there are specific Laws covering them.

Each of these 22 Laws has a natural nemesis, a matching Crime they seek to address.

For example, layers of indecision-makers, armies of no-men, constant changes of direction and glacial approval processes are guilty of marring, distracting and diluting *The Law of Simplicity.*

A creative culture where one-off, in-joke ads are rewarded with creative awards can undermine *The Law of Consistency;* and so on.

Indeed, many of the world's greatest communicators spend most of their time not so much practising and refining the Laws of great advertising, but rather attending to the problems caused by the perpetrators of Crimes against good advertising.

Here are 10 examples of random violence against great advertising that come to mind immediately.

1. The Crime of Research

Anita Roddick, founder of The Body Shop, once described research as being "like looking in the rear-view mirror of a fast-moving car."

More profitable ideas have died, needlessly, due to the mindless, scorekeeping-use of research than any other weapon.

Research and destroy.

Pre-testing advertising concepts often turns potent magic into patent rubbish. It makes the inhuman assumption that what people say and what they do is somehow the same thing.

Sometimes, advertisers argue: "We use only it as a 'disaster check'."

This is really managing for failure.

It's clear that consumers make brand choices intuitively, so asking them how likely they are to buy a brand obviously isn't going to give accurate results.

It's equally clear that, as long as there are insecure clients, there will be ongoing concept research.

Yet, in going down this path so pathologically, the industry has managed to stifle innovative communication at the same time as technology delivers container loads of product-parity to advertise.

It's not only advertising, of course.

Hollywood shows a movie before its release to a bevy of hairdressers, truck drivers, secretaries and labourers in Dogsbody, Arkansas, who all declare that the death of the hero in the final reel is unacceptable. Bowing to this, the movie is changed so there is a happy ending.

Let's face it, if research worked, Hollywood would never fail (fewer than six out of 10 movies make money, for the record; In fact, their ROI is between 4 to 5% — they'd be more profitable putting their money in a bank account).

UK trend forecasters Martin Raymond and Chris Sanderson spoke out against research when visiting Australia recently: "Focus groups? Forget them. The only thing a customer tells you is what you want them to tell you. Don't trust them."

2. The Crime of Logic

Most advertisers are preoccupied with finding the logically right answer, instead of the emotionally real answer.

Many are scared of risk. Even worse, they're reluctant to go with their instinct. They shy away — even if they sense it will work — because they can't prove it. The result is that sharp, non-lineal ideas are routinely blunted under the pressure of management's zealous rationality. The problem is that advertising creativity isn't a linear process, by definition, so all the logic and cognitive analysis that has led to the moment when the brief is handed over to the creative people is often of limited use.

An original idea is the desired outcome, and originality is a leap sideways from any of the steps that precede it.

Emotionally powerful ideas must be allowed to overcome the relentlessly rational process.

If you want to be a successful advertiser, my advice is: don't judge ideas with your head, judge them with your heart.

Feel about it.

Don't think about it.

Real people aren't *thinking* that hard when they look at advertising, and neither should you.

The heart tells you if you have been touched, made to laugh or cry, or whether the idea is hackneyed, empty or dull.

The eye is meant to see things.
The soul is here for its own joy …
Mysteries are not to be solved.
The eye goes blind
When it only wants to see why.
— Jalal al-Din Rumi, 13th-Century Sufi poet

The problem of analysis paralysis infects other professions too. I once met a stand-up comedian who told me how his occupation ruined the ability to laugh: "If I hear a good joke," he said seriously, "I don't laugh, I think: 'Mm, very funny … but *why?*'"

Analyse this: Regardless of how logically "on track" it is, unless the idea is emotionally compelling, it won't begin to solve your marketing problem.

And the product won't sell.

So, only when you're sure the ad is engaging emotionally should you logically process whether the idea fits the brief, or the brand values or even, dare I say, the budget.

(The animated film, *Finding Nemo*, was one of the biggest hits in the US in 2003. At the time, a number of trainspotters pointed out that it's not technically possible for a fish to be swallowed by a whale and then sprayed out its blowhole — there is no physical connection between a leviathan's digestive tract and windpipe.

But Hollywood wasn't training gastroenterologists, was it? They're trying to be popular, not precise. They know there's a place for imaginative leaps of faith when capturing hearts.)

Your advertising process should be a structured search for a wonderful accident of circumstance, the creation of something new and powerful, potent enough to make interesting things happen.

Sometimes you have to elevate the idea's importance even over the original strategic thinking.

Big ideas don't always fit the brief; usually, they are bigger than the original brief.

Big ideas generate unforeseen opportunities. They can change the nature or focus of an entire company.

I once heard a professional garden designer lament, to some of his clients, "It's an inconvenience that their trees grow — they need to learn to relinquish control and let the garden evolve to something unexpected and wonderfully bigger than anything that would have gone to a logical plan."

3. The Crime of Familiarity

Familiarity breeds inertia.

Familiarity breeds contempt.

And it repeats clichés.

While on the subject of being predictable, I'll quote the great Bill Bernbach (after all, doesn't everybody?): *"What was effective one day, for that very reason, will not be effective the next, because it has lost the maximum impact of originality."*

Brands were invented to achieve differentiation, yet clients crazily demand: "Please give me something like blah-blah-blah ..." Problem is, when blah blah blah was done originally, there was nothing like it at all.

Rid yourself of any preconceptions of how the solution should look. Most ads blend because they are based on previous experience; traditional wisdom is too traditional.

Speechwriter and author Don Watson asked: "When was the last time you heard a politician use words that rang with truth and meaning? ... Do your eyes glaze over when you read a letter from your bank? When your employer tells you to make a commitment going forwards, or speaks of enhancing the bottom line, does your mind shut down?"

Ambiguity and surprise are what force our interest.

As the poet, Ezra Pound, wrote: "Make it new for me."

4. The Crime of Self Importance

There's an apocryphal story about a US TV executive who admitted: "We make programs for the people we fly over." This same high handedness infects many major marketers. My local cinema doesn't have "ads" running before the main feature anymore; instead, they have what they bill as "pre-movie entertainment."

If only.

It's been said that most marketers have become too used to viewing people as consumers, as if ordinary people live life in a race for precious resources. In fact, most folk would rather bond in a supportive community, than compete in a survivalist competition (which is actually more the cut and thrust mindset of the business world).

The Nilewide.com newsletter points out that many business leaders are of an age where all they basically had to do in their day was to get people to buy stuff at a time when most families didn't have most of the things they wanted anyway.

Business liked believing it was in control.

Propped up with self-importance, most companies have a strong hierarchical set up, the kind learnt in the army to run in a very macho way. Communications were a monologue.

The business of persuasion must now, however, become less coercive and more discursive.

Mass-market advertising that used to bombard, push and solicit, must now learn to attract. Seduce. Engage. The feminisation of marketing, it's been called, with its way of expressing marketing dialogues is relationship-driven and seductive. Ironically, this will be the most effective way of achieving the macho objective of control over customer preferences or attitudes.

You shouldn't be trying to teach people facts about your product; you should be trying to create an emotional belief about your product. Tomorrow's successful brands will add value through reassurance, shared emotions, and non-rational meaning. The evolution, or perhaps it's a revolution to some, is from so-called "ingredients brands" to "solution brands."

Or, to put it in less self-important language: People want to know about their beautiful flowers, not about the phosphate levels in your manure.

5. The Crimes against Humanity

Advertising often inhabits its own world of glossy, over-polished, buffed, idealised and unrealistic achievement. It's so "cheesy."

As the world becomes more commercial, there's an increased yearning for authenticity, human scale, slow food, reading groups, natural fibres and organic vegetables. The paying public wants to see advertising that is more empathetic. This is about having the intellectual honesty to be more realistic. Unless you "reach out and touch" somebody, no one will reach for your brand.

Film guru, Robert McKee, teaches that if you want global success, be culturally specific and universally human.

It was ironic that, during the massive power failure that affected the north western part of the US and parts of Canada in 2003, it was for many New Yorkers the first time they could see stars — the Big Dipper, in fact — which, for the rest of the world, is one of the brightest constellations in the sky.

I mean it's easy to feel very sophisticated but yet be totally out of touch with the big, important things in life.

And what is real? I got these basic human truths from English strategist, David Keig, at Keig & Co., Australia:

Nobody trusts someone who can be all things to all people or just says what they know you want to hear.

We all like to be surprised.

Our friends aren't identical to us, nor do we want them to be.

We hate it when someone keeps saying "I know what you like."

We get bored when people always look and act the same.

We feel uncomfortable when people behave out of character.

We hate false interest and fake or hollow courtesies.

We hate people who have only one joke in their repertoire and keep telling it repeatedly.

We dislike people who take things too seriously.

We hate to be disturbed when relaxing or concentrating on something.

We hate to be patronised.

We hate false sincerity.

We will forgive mistakes…up to a point.

We dislike jealousy.

We like to learn from others.

We like to share experiences.

We like to chat and just stay in touch.

We hate people who overstay their welcome or are too ardent in seeking friendship.

Now, ask the question: "Why should brands be any different in the way they behave?"

Then, ask the question: "Is my brand as real as that?"

The odds are that it isn't and, in the quest for likeability and trustworthiness and so on, the brand's personality has become just too squeaky clean and artificial to be real.

Too good to be true.

So, neither good nor truthful.

6. The Crime of Atheism

Sinners repent; advertising works like magic.

Like magic, you have to believe in it first. If you don't believe in advertising's transformational power, then you won't make effective advertising. So why then are you incurring its cost?

One of the reasons advertising isn't as good as it should be, is that too few marketers truly believe in its efficacy. This leads to short-term imperatives taking precedence over (ultimately more profitable) brand building.

Marketing is supposed to be about the discovery of a commercially rich human insight, which is then vividly realised in creative execution. Yet, many marketing departments spend their money and much of their working lives "ticking all the boxes" – this isn't being a professional communicator; rather, it's the surest way to enforce rigorous standards of mediocrity, guaranteeing the production of bland, uninspired blancmange.

So turn your profession into your passion or risk turning your brand into a commodity. You'll need to recognise the essential values of the intangible: passion, sensuality and story.

If your goal is to create belief in your brand, then start by believing nothing is impossible.

The original scientist, Sir Isaac Newton, had a lucky horseshoe over his front door. This shocked his zealously rational associates, who demanded that surely he did not believe in such things?

Newton answered: "No; but I hear it works anyway."

Try to have faith. Look at the miracles that have been wrought in earlier times.

"Boldness," wrote Goethe, "has genius, power and magic in it."

Nowhere is that more true than in advertising.

7. The Crime of Strangulation by Data

Advertisers are avalanched with data and yet increasingly starved of understanding, connection, magnetism and humanity.

Data is not knowledge.

Knowledge is not necessarily insight.

And insight is not yet an idea.

The problem is rarely a failure of information, but of receptivity, a failure of ideology even. There is a pathology of measurement in today's advertising departments, an obsession with reducing all things to a set of "objective" numbers. The problem with this is that numbers seem to give decision-makers a false sense of precision. Marketers get mesmerised by it.

Advertising, however, is incitement. It's the tone, the style, the charm, the presentation, and the timing that's effective.

It's more manner than matter.

Or data.

In short, it's better to be approximately right than precisely and coldly wrong.

Aoccdrnig to rscheearch at an Elingsh Uinervtisy it deosn't mttaer in waht order the ltteers in a word are, the only iprmoetnt thing is that the frist and lsat ltteer is at the rghit pclae. The rset can be a total mses and oyu can still raed it wuothit porbelm. This is bcuseae we do not raed ervey lteter by itself but the word as a wlohe.

Get the starting point right, know the end you've in sight and make the middle interesting; don't sweat the minutae.

As Nicholas Samstag quipped in his wonderful book, *Bamboozled*: Like seduction, you know when your idea's been successful or unsuccessful; in good or bad taste.

Don't be deluded; neither seduction nor great advertising can be accomplished with any technique based primarily on numbers.

Instead, leave a gap for the mind to accelerate into.

Look for a pebble on the beach, polish it and mount it, so it catches the light.

8. The Crime of Interference

This is the insanity of barking when you have a dog.

Yes, advertising is a "collaborative art"; but that's not the same thing as decisions made by committee. Worse, many make it an adversarial process, which inevitably leads to compromise.

Advertising, like Hollywood, is a nervous industry. I understand the producer of the original *Scream* movie wanted to shoot seven alternatives to the scream mask, so he could decide later which one the murderer would wear.

Too often, in the misguided interests of "relationship building," otherwise well-meaning clients are allowed to unwittingly unravel a precisely balanced idea with the infamous "pecked to death by ducks" syndrome, even after the concept has been approved.

Once there has been a successful pre-production meeting, the client really shouldn't see the commercial again until it is finished. That's the only way of judging it objectively.

Clients should be discouraged from sitting on the shoulders of their creatives like a nagging conscience (are we there yet?). The creatives need to be given room to breathe life into the solution.

Advertisers belittle themselves trying to be second-rate writers or directors; rather, they should cast themselves in the more nurturing role of an impresario, which, is defined in my dictionary as:

(1) a producer or promoter of commercial entertainment ventures

(2) somebody in charge of an opera or ballet company who is responsible for business affairs, contracting artists, and commissioning new works

(3) a showman

The greatest impresario who ever lived, was Diaghilev, the director of the Russian Ballet Russes, who tapped into the talents of Picasso, Braque, Matisse, Prokofiev, Stravinsky, Fokine, Massine, and Cocteau. His ability was to know who was great, gather them all in, and famously say to them: "Etonne-moi (astonish me)."

The alternative is to risk over-balancing a fine-tuned piece, and ruining the effect because the agency was too browbeaten or obsequious to stop you.

It reminds me of the time when boxer Tony Mundine was trained to deliver a specially written 'quotable quote' for a big press conference; unfortunately, he followed up the catchy line by adding something of his own that just happened to ruin the total effect:

Holding up his clenched fist for the cameras and reporters, he was coached to say: "This right hand has put more still life on canvas than Rembrandt..."

Unfortunately, just as the reporters were scribbling down the line, Mundine then added, in a loud and overheard stage whisper to his manager: "... anyway, who the fuck's Rembrandt?"

Unfortunately, as the great HG Wells wrote: "No passion in the world is equal to the passion to alter someone's draft."
(ED: Sorry, you'll have to change that.)

9. The Crime of the Pitch

The new business pitch is perhaps the most abused of all the entrenched processes in the industry. Many agencies resent them; after all, do the same clients get accountants to pitch for every project? Do they get roomfuls of different law firms to present alternative defences for court cases?

Giving out free ideas and strategy in creative pitches is a drain on agency resources and morale. Often it's little more than a stretched-out process of the client experimenting with marketing strategy or reinforcing a master – slave relationship with their agencies.

Fear is a lousy climate in which to grow great work.

It's been described as the same set of power tools as calling 7a.m. meetings and constantly conducting business outside business hours. I know this sounds crazy, but clients should try to be more intuitive, more trusting, and more ethical when looking for a business partner — if only because a subservient and compliant lap dog just won't do the job these days.

Agencies, of course, have encouraged this behaviour. Jumping through hoops and switching to vaudeville to convince clients of their professional insights is a troubled concept.

The successful agency – client relationship is about partnership, revenue-sharing and incentive. Agencies work better when they are motivated, not when they're reduced to a cost-based generic supplier.

Which leads me to:

10. The Crime of Commoditization of the Creative Product

Years of wheeling-dealing and creative price-cutting by agencies have devalued ideas. This was a mortal sin.

"If you eliminate creative as a discriminator between agencies, network groups can sell bundled-up services at a discount price," pointed out the UK's Lord Saatchi in a recent interview. "Network groups have a vested interest ... (in wanting) creative to become a commodity."

But creativity is the essence of advertising salesmanship.

Accountability needs to work both ways; auditors are as common as art directors in some agency corridors, but can the role of long-term brand building be properly measured yet?

An idea like "Think Different" written on a pad dramatically changes the value of that piece of paper.

INDEX